KU-365-832

OTHER TITLES IN THE SERIES

Alternative Kilns
Ian Gregory

Ceramics with Mixed Media
Joy Bosworth

Ceramics and Print
Paul Scott

Coiling
Michael Hardy

Colouring Clay
Jo Connell

Crystalline Glazes
Diane Creber

The Electric Kiln
Harry Fraser

Glazes Cone 6
Michael Bailey

Handbuilding
Michael Hardy

Impressed and Incised Ceramics
Coll Minogue

Kiln Building
Ian Gregory

Large-scale Ceramics
Jim Robison

Lettering on Ceramics
Mary White

Low Firing and Burnishing
Sumi Von Dassow

Oriental Glazes
Michael Bailey

Paper Clay
Rosette Gault

Porcelain
Jack Doherty

Raku
John Mathieson

Resist and Masking Techniques
Peter Beard

Setting Up a Pottery Workshop
Alistair Young

Single Firing
Fran Tristram

Slipcasting
Sasha Wardell

Stoneware
Richard Dewar

Soda Glazing
Ruthanne Tudball

Throwing Pots
Phil Rogers

Wall Pieces
Dominique Bivar Segurado

CERAMIC JEWELLERY

Joy Bosworth

The American Ceramic Society • Ohio

B L O O M S B U R Y
LONDON • NEW DELHI • NEW YORK • SYDNEY

Dedication

To Bruce, Daniel, Jasmine and Nancy with all my love.

FRONTISPIECE: Joy Bosworth, *Two Twisted Bracelets*, 2008. Forged silver wire with raku bead, dia: 8cm (3in.) diameter. *Photo: Dan Bosworth.*

Bloomsbury Visual Arts
An imprint of Bloomsbury Publishing Plc

50 Bedford Square
London
WC1B 3DP
UK

1385 Broadway
New York
NY 10018
USA

www.bloomsbury.com

Bloomsbury is a registered trade mark of Bloomsbury Publishing Plc

© Joy Bosworth 2010

CIP Catalogue records for this book are available from the British Library and the US Library of Congress.

First published in 2010 by A & C Black Publishers Limited
Reprinted by Bloomsbury Visual Arts in 2014

Published simultaneously in the USA by
The American Ceramic Society
600 N. Cleveland Ave., Suite 210,
Westerville, Ohio 43082

All rights reserved. No part of this publication may be reproduced in any form or by any means – graphic, electronic or mechanical, including photocopying, recording, taping or information storage and retrieval systems – without the prior permission in writing of the publishers.

No responsibility for loss caused to any individual or organization acting on or refraining from action as a result of the material in this publication can be accepted by Bloomsbury or the author.

Joy Bosworth has asserted her right under the Copyright, Design and Patents Act 1988 to be identified as the author of this work.

ISBN: PB: 978-1-4081-0637-2
US ed: 978-1-574-98305-0

Typeset in 10 on 12 1/2pt Photina
Book design by Susan McIntyre
Cover design by Sutchinda Thompson

Printed and bound in China

CAUTION: Operating high-temperature kilns and using blow torches and burners are inherently dangerous activities. Please use adequate safeguards when attempting any of the techniques and activities described in this book because you assume all associated risks. The publishers and author cannot be held responsible in the case of accident or injury resulting from any procedure or instruction discussed here.

Contents

Preface

This book aims to inform and inspire those who may wish to explore jewellery and body adornment which uses clay with or without other materials. By developing new skills with different materials it may be possible to further develop your work and broaden its scope.

The chapter on designing is directed at those who have not yet designed their own pieces (or wished to develop their practices), and suggests ways you can approach making work of a more individual nature.

The book describes simple clay techniques of forming and decorating, together with simple ideas of how ceramic pieces can be made into jewellery. Jewellery findings can be made from metal or other materials, and a few simple examples are explained and illustrated. Some additional metalwork techniques will help when making ceramic pieces into jewellery. All kinds of manufactured jewellery findings are available to buy, and the examples given demonstrate how such off-the-peg findings can be combined adventurously with handmade findings to integrate ceramic elements into jewellery.

Acknowledgements

I would like to thank Terry Hunt, Deputy Head of the School of Jewellery, Birmingham City University, for allowing me to work with BA students on a project for this book. Thanks also to all those makers who have been generous enough to contribute images of their work and descriptions of their techniques and inspirations. Thanks to Bruce for his computer skills, Dan for his photography and Yvonne Ogilvie-Hardy for the use of her long shed in which to work. Thanks also to Linda Lambert and Alison Stace for giving me the opportunity to write another book and for helping to bring it into existence.

Introduction

Body adornment is one of the oldest art forms; throughout history, people all over the world have decorated their bodies in one way or another. In its earliest and most primitive forms, clay and earth pigments were smeared or painted on the body to adorn it and to create mystery or theatre during rituals. Beads made from a variety of materials were one of the simplest forms of jewellery, and were also used as currency, to confer status and to ward off bad spirits. Historically, amulets, charms and talismans were widely worn to protect orifices such as the nose, ears or mouth, or at the extremities of ankles or wrists to ward off evil spirits.

Body adornment, an integral part of important rites of passage, was used to display, adorn and protect during various phases, stages and conditions of mankind. The impressive jewellery gallery of the Victoria and Albert Museum in London divides exhibits into the following categories: birth and fertility, childhood and survival, love and fidelity, beliefs and superstitions, death and mourning, and wealth and status.

During the Middle Ages in Europe, jewellery was worn to signify religious devotion, love and status, or for medicinal purposes. Some thought precious stones could protect against harm from those whose envy might affect their well-being. Amazingly, some thought precious stones could promote world peace and reconciliation.

During the 16th century, precious metals and gemstones flooded into Europe after the conquest of South America by the Spaniards. Two centuries later, in France in the years immediately following the Revolution, jewellery was frowned upon as being the symbol of wealth and rank, causing jewellers to move away from Paris to other parts of Europe. However, the coronation of Napoleon and Josephine as Emperor and Empress reversed that trend,[1] because they embellished their bodies with jewellery and clothes made from rich fabrics, influencing fashions.

By the 1860s, manufactured jewellery, made by machine from base metals that were gold-plated to imitate precious jewellery, was widespread throughout Europe, making it more affordable. By the 1900s René Lalique (1860–1945) was demonstrating that jewellery made from common materials such as horn and glass could command high prices because of the design and skill displayed, rather than the inherent value of the materials. His work elevated the artistic quality of jewellery, in the process highlighting a fact that still applies to a lot of traditional jewellery being made today, namely that the more valuable the stone or precious metal used, the less imaginative the setting.

Non-precious jewellery has been given many different names to justify its existence: fantasy jewellery, costume jewellery, travel jewellery, *bijoux de couture* (designer jewellery), haute couture accessories, or less complimentary descriptions such as *vrais bijoux en toc* (true second-rate jewellery) or imitation jewellery. It has, at certain times, been chic to wear cheap or trashy jewellery, and the exaggerated designs possible with cheaper materials have even influenced precious jewellery styles.

The term 'fantasy jewel', denoting non-precious materials producing imitation jewellery, was coined in 1873 when the first trade union for costume jewellery was formed in Paris. At the beginning of the 20th century costume jewellery began to be designed as part of an ensemble in haute couture. This *bijoux de couture* used the latest technologies. Coco Chanel (1883–1971) designed extravagant jewellery as accessories for her fashion designs, her *vrais bijoux en toc* (as she described it) contrasting with and complimenting her severe, high-quality clothing. The Gripoix company, which made her pieces, worked also for theatre and costume balls organised by people like Paul Poiret (1879–1944).[2] In 2008 Chanel launched a ring in 18K white gold and diamonds with glazed ceramic components, further blurring the boundaries between precious and costume jewellery.

Around 1925, Elsa Schiaparelli (1890–1973) collaborated with Salvador Dalí and Méret Oppenheim to design pieces which she thought of as 'travel jewellery'. 'Phoney became chic', states Carles Codina in *The New Jewelry: Contemporary Materials and Techniques*. Some women bought precious jewellery precisely because it was as flamboyant in style as the 'phoney' costume jewellery. In the 1930s and '40s Salvador Dalí made 'pieces of extreme exuberance

which both fascinate and unsettle us because of the delirious wastefulness of the gold and precious gems used in their creation.'[3]

The Ruskin Pottery, based in Smethwick in the West Midlands, was well-known internationally for its art nouveau vases with glazes influenced by the Chinese. It also made roundels or plaques, which were incorporated into metal-mounted wares – such as silver-mounted brooches, boxes and fire screens – by metal manufacturers including Tiffany. The Ruskin Pottery closed in 1933 after sales dropped in the early 1930s due to the economic depression caused by the stock market crash of 1929. The Depression also caused the production of precious jewellery to fall dramatically, which naturally led to an increase in the production of costume jewellery. It was not until the 1950s, however, that costume jewellery designers were recognised and their names were first seen on their work.

In 1961, the V&A in London held a joint exhibition with the Worshipful Company of Goldsmiths, described as 'the world's first display of modern jewellery'. 'Its purpose was to revive the depressed British jewellery trade, which had suffered badly from the war, postwar austerity and purchase tax.'[4] It has more recently opened an imaginative contemporary gallery space to display its jewellery collection spanning 3000 years.

Contemporary jewellers work in a wide variety of ways, some within the confines of an ancient craft, others in areas more akin to fine art or sculpture which challenge expectations and traditions. Jewellery design has become

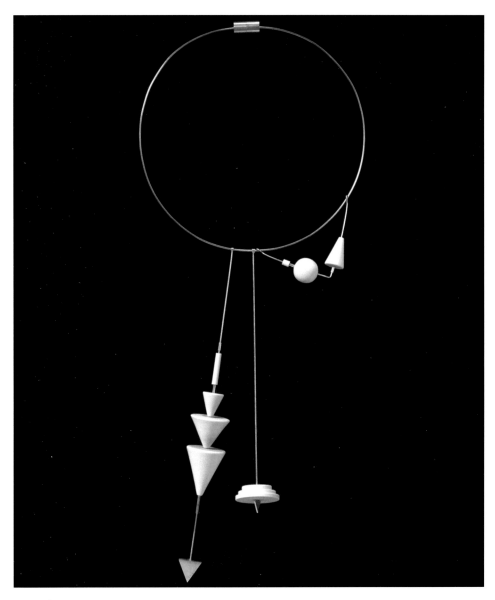

Wendy Ramshaw, necklace, 1982. Gold with silver catch and hand-turned beads of jasper.
Photo © V&A Images/Victoria and Albert Museum, London, with permission from the artist.

less about the slavish repetition of the past and more about the idea and the materials from which it is made. Contemporary jewellers have thus felt increasingly able to respond to innovative materials, to set trends, to question the status of jewellery and to comment on political or social issues.

Wendy Ramshaw, who designed a collection of jewellery for Wedgwood in the 1980s, explored the idea of combining their coloured stoneware

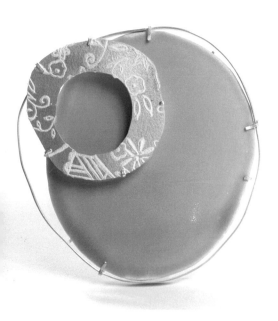

Kathryn Partington, *Silence Brooch*, 2007. Glazed bone china and silver with raised pigment, 7.5 × 8 cm (3 × 3⅛ in.). *Photo: Gareth Partington.*

with precious metals and gemstones to make jewellery; it was an unusual combination of materials at the time and still looks contemporary three decades later. The collection was launched with a show at the V&A in 1982 and is featured in Wedgwood's new jewellery gallery, which was opened in 2008.

Kathryn Partington, who has worked with Wedgwood more recently as a surface-pattern designer, has also now started working on jewellery pieces, but in a looser way than Ramshaw, combining bone china with silver. She creates textured surfaces on bone china and silver, which respond to the surface pattern found on an old Japanese box. The fragile bone-china medallions are protected by silver findings with claws to hold them in place.

Numerous books have been published to comment on and inspire new design, whilst art colleges and universities offer courses to teach traditional skills and to promote new approaches and work. In the UK in the 1970s, the Crafts Council (and later this involved the Arts Council) was set up as a national agency for contemporary crafts, with its aim being 'to position the UK as the best in the world for making, seeing and collecting contemporary craft'. International competitions such as the Jerwood Jewellery Prize, and selected exhibitions such as Schmuck (which has been going for 50 years), 'encourage and promote the work of new jewellers', and also show new work by established makers. Ralph Turner, who curated Schmuck in 2008, looks for ideas first, then 'context, lucidity and dexterity, along with quality and fitness for purpose'.[5]

Ceramics is being included by some contemporary jewellers as part of a large and varied palette of different non-precious materials – a range that also comprises plastic, sealing wax, felt, paper, plaster, ferrous metals, rubber and wood – which are used instead of or as well as precious metals and gems. Jewellers engage in a dialogue with materials as a means of expanding their visual language. Ralph Turner states that, 'much like music, jewellery, at its best, can express a wide range of emotions and meanings. As an art form it has the ability to engage with contemporary issues – both social and political ...'.[6] Examples of this are Aneta Regel Deleu's *Volcanic Ring* (see p.94) and the work of Ruudt Peters (see p.101).

Jewellers like Sebastian Buescher make work which fits into this new art jewellery category. He tells me:

Sebastian Buescher, *Blood Sweat and Tears*, 2008. Necklace: oxide-stained earthenware fired to 1100°C (2030°F), garnet, steel, wool and plastic, 950 mm (37 in.), Amsterdam. *Photo: Sebastian Buescher. Reproduced by kind permission of Galerie Rob Koudijs, Amsterdam.*

Lauren Griffiths, *Memories*, 2009. Porcelain, silver, sand, glass jar with cork; 95 x 43mm (3¾ x 1¾ in.). *Photo: Graham Bradbury.*

'Recently, I have been exploring the invisible energy within second-hand objects, natural phenomena such as ghosts, and the meaning and purpose of myself as a human being.' He seeks to achieve 'a deeper understanding of the world, a raw layer of reality which is carefully hidden beneath the surface, invisible to the naked eye. What we see is surely not what we get. Quite on the contrary, what we see is only an illusion, and my work attempts to question and taunt these, exposing the fleshy reality beneath.'

Lauren Griffiths's work is at the crossover point between sculpture and jewellery. Her beautiful, delicate objects, which she sees as fragments of memory, are made from porcelain (for its pure, fossil-like qualities) and silver, and presented in specimen jars to 'preserve' and display them. Fragile yet precious, some of the pieces could be worn.

Contemporary ceramics makers known primarily for other work in ceramics have realised that many people wear jewellery who might not buy pots or ceramic sculpture; so by turning to jewellery, they are broadening their market and reaching a wider audience. Economic reasons are also a consideration, as making jewellery expands the price structure of their saleable products. The fashion for large-size costume jewellery has also given ceramics makers an opening into a new market. Another factor is the efficient (and therefore cost-effective) use of kiln space, where smaller items can fit in and around other larger work. Steve Sedgwick makes brooches, like test tiles, as a way of exploring surfaces and glazes for larger pieces. Alisdair and Sally MacDonell first started to make brooches that were within the price range of children, and also to allow people to buy a small piece of their work. They have found that encouraging people to buy a low-cost introductory piece like this draws people into buying their larger pieces in subsequent years.

[1] Linda Grant, 'V & A's New Jewellery Gallery: Rocks of Ages', *Sunday Telegraph* supplement, 11 May 2008.

[2] Carles Codina i Armengol, *The New Jewelery: Contemporary Materials and Techniques* (Lark Books, 2005).

[3] Carles Codina i Armengol, *The New Jewelery: Contemporary Materials and Techniques* (Lark Books, 2005).

[4] Linda Grant, 'V & A's New Jewellery Gallery: Rocks of Ages', *Sunday Telegraph* supplement, 11 May 2008.

[5] Ralph Turner, Statement in catalogue *Schmuck*, 2008, Editor Wolfgang Lösche, GHM-Gesellschaft, 2008.

[6] Ralph Turner, Statement in catalogue *Schmuck*, 2008, Editor Wolfgang Lösche, GHM-Gesellschaft, 2008.

Chapter 1

Design considerations for jewellery

How, when, why and by whom the body adornment will be worn are the first considerations when designing. Considerations of size, scale, types of materials and function will all be affected by the answers to those questions. If the work is commissioned, then some, if not all, of these decisions will be clear. However, if the project is self-generated, these answers may emerge as research is being done, and one's own personal creativity will have a bearing upon the areas explored. The chapter on findings later in the book will help you when considering function, while the types of materials and methods you use in bringing a piece together all contribute to the end result.

Contemporary-art body adornment has become very dynamic, experimental and thought-provoking; questioning its relationship to the wearer, it is more about theatre or sculpture than function. But if you wish to make something to be worn, whatever the occasion, then function cannot be ignored.

Clay is hard but brittle, so it needs to be shaped into a form which has strength (i.e. a tube or a sphere), and should be thick enough to withstand knocks or else surrounded by a metal finding to protect it. If the form is small and strong enough (e.g. a small bead),

then a lower earthenware firing can be used. The Egyptians made very low-fired, Egyptian-paste amulets which have survived for thousands of years. High firing and the use of glaze will give a piece strength, although, as with any ceramics, breakage may occur if it is dropped onto a hard surface.

Holes should not be too near the edge of a piece, and should be made with a suitable tool when the piece is leatherhard in case cracks appear during making or drying that will be a weak spot when the piece is worn.

Shrinkage must always be taken into consideration. Clay shrinks during drying and firing, sometimes by as much as 16% (although 10–12% is more normal), so it is best to buy or make findings only after the ceramic part of the piece has had its final firing, or to take this shrinkage into account when buying or making findings. It is always better to make more ceramic elements than you need for the design, to allow for breakage or disappointing results from the firing.

When first making jewellery, you may find it easier to copy historic or contemporary pieces, making variations on a theme. Whilst being influenced by the work of others, the pieces made will nevertheless always have something of the maker in them, and will rarely be exact replicas. However, the more adventurous or experienced may wish to find a more individual style and to start designing one-off pieces. So here are some of the things to consider when designing.

Ideas do not come out of the blue; they are developed from visual, contextual and material-sampling research. By researching other makers (contextual research), developing the ability to look and see opportunities for design ideas wherever you are, collecting images and materials (visual research), and experimenting with techniques and materials, a 'bank' of possibilities will be amassed for future use. This is how your own creative identity or style emerges. It is important to develop your skills and knowledge of different materials alongside the research, or the designs you want to make will outstrip your ability to make them. Sometimes, experimenting with materials and skills will suggest other contextual and visual research that you might not have considered relevant. It is an ongoing, two-way process.

Drawing/visual communication for 3D design

Photography, drawing, painting, photocopying, collage and materials samples are all ways of conveying design ideas. Here are some of the considerations, when using sketch/work books or when making a design sheet. Both sketchbooks and design sheets can be produced in a variety of materials and techniques which may include drawing, painting, photography, collage, materials sampling and experimentation. Sketchbooks should be used to gather visual research and to work through ideas and design problems. They should be exciting and experimental although some ideas may not be as successful as others. Design sheets should have visual impact, should communicate the final ideas – how they work and how they will be worn on the body and 'sell the ideas' to a potential buyer.

One approach to a design project: visual research and images on a theme

Photographic reference books of the kind you can find in art libraries and good bookshops can act as source books for design and may inspire your own search for visual references. The contents of these books may be organised into themes of colour, texture, form and/or structure, which may highlight the way contrasts and juxtapositions can either shock and disturb or be complementary and soothing.

At first glance topics such as fish, flowers and landscapes are fairly obvious, but if you examine close-ups and other details of these subjects, what begin to emerge are more abstract questions of colour, texture, form and structure.

Inspiration for designing – campervan bodywork. *Photo: Lydia Feast.*

Betina's Rust applied with a sponge first, then turquoise mix with glaze 12. Take off with sponge, applied more 12 using toothbrush with Bettina's rust again.

Turquoise mixed with 12.

Iron oxide mixed with painting solution. Applied using plastic sheet.

Dipped in water. Oil-based painting solution with iron oxide.

Dipped in water. Oil-based painting solution + iron oxide.

Glaze 16 with Betina's Rust (15).

Turquoise mixed with glaze 12 plus Betina's Rust.

Lydia Feast, test samples and experiments. *Photo: Graham Bradbury.*

Glaze recipe 12 (oxidised)

'George's' 1260°C (2300°F) Matt White

Feldspar Potash	1000g
China Clay	500g
Dolomite	450g
Whiting	70g

Glaze recipe 15 (oxidised) *

'Betina's Rust' Shiny Rust Glaze with Black Speckles where thick 1260°C (2300°F)

Potash Feldspar	580g
Quartz or Flint	180g
Bone Ash	80g
China Clay	80g
Talc	80g
Red Iron Oxide	100g

Glaze recipe 16 (oxidised) *

Turquoise 1260°C (2300°F)

Feldspar Potash	49g
Barium carbonate	27g
Whiting	14g
Ball clay	9g
Bentonite	1g
Copper carbonate	2.5g

* Originally Stephen Murfitt glazes, from The Glaze Book *published by Thames & Hudson, 2002.*

Lydia Feast, jewellery maquettes. Top three: stoneware-fired fragments with oxide and Lydia's glazes No. 12, 15 and 16, and found cotton-covered buttons with rusty washer and rusty iron wire. Bottom four maquettes: porcelain buttons, blue enamelled copper buttons with rusty iron wire and sheet fragments. *Photo: Graham Bradbury.*

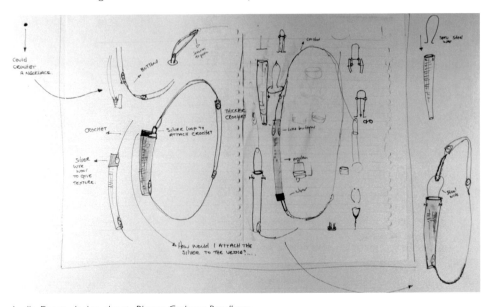

Lydia Feast, design sheet. *Photo: Graham Bradbury.*

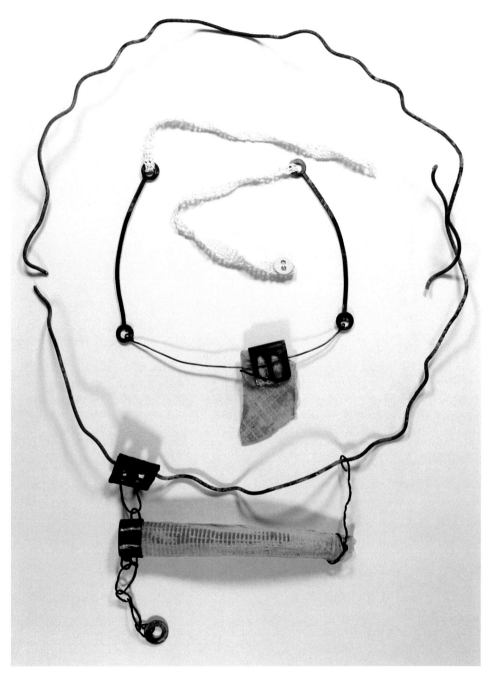

Lydia Feast, neckpiece maquettes, 2008. Rusty iron wire and fragments with oxidised copper element formed and soldered, rusty washers, buff stoneware-fired tube and fragment with turquiose stoneware glaze and iron oxide, cotton crocheted tape and found cotton-covered buttons.
Photo: Graham Bradbury.

Other, less obvious subjects can be found by looking at details of buildings, distressed surfaces, lines, crosses or circles found in the environment. Almost anything you find of interest can be developed into a theme. By starting to explore such themes, you may start to develop surprising ideas.

Lydia Feast started designing for her body adornment pieces using images of details from the bodywork of a camper van. The long thin shapes in the photo (see p.14) became important not only as a flat detail but also as a tube shape, a strong form through which the other materials or findings can be threaded. The photo on p.17 shows that Lydia developed the idea further by making maquettes, using the found materials themselves as part of the design. This way of working suggested design ideas which could not have developed in any other way. The twists in the reclaimed wire (shown on p.17) could not have been thought of unless the found materials themselves had been used in the designing process.

Testing with clay types, textures and glazes is also part of the designing process, and in the photo on p.15 a number of tests by Lydia Feast can be seen to achieve qualities she has seen in the bodywork images and the found pieces of rusty metal.

Drawings of different options and ideas help the development of the project: it is possible to work out many visual and practical problems through drawing alone, without having to make all the various permutations.

Experiments with materials samples, photocopying and art materials enable the realisation of new ideas developed from photographic visual research. This materials-handling and other 2D work may lead to more photography as the ideas develop. Also, the project is further informed by visits to good libraries, museums and galleries, to carry out more research into those contemporary and historic makers whose work echoes the qualities being explored.

Materials-handling experiments may suggest new ways of manipulating the clay, which can be made to mimic other media. Practical and design ideas can be worked out on paper, some being discarded and some further developed, so that only the better ones are actually made.

Another approach to design: A techniques-led project

The manipulation of selected materials by cutting, joining and rejoining can free up the designing and thought processes and promote new ideas. The materials-handling experiments will begin to become abstract, being partly about the qualities of the materials used and partly about jewellery. Collections of materials not usually considered for jewellery, both found and bought, can be a good starting point for jewellery design. Materials like coloured or white paper, card, plastic, fabric, newspaper, yarns, paints, crayons, photocopies, found materials like cocktail sticks, drinking straws, electrical wire, buttons, packaging materials, deconstructed urban artefacts found in skips, etc. can inspire a design. Collage, paint and drawing techniques can be used to explore possibilities as well as the manipulation of materials.

Making maquettes or models out of these materials may free up your

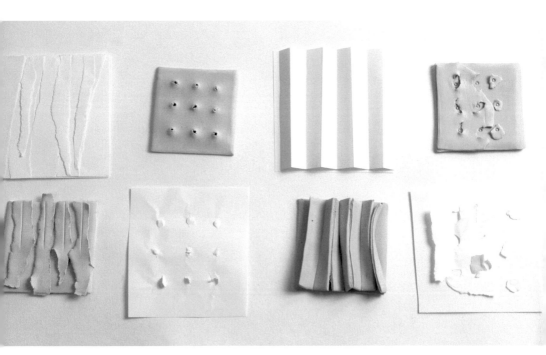

ABOVE Joy Bosworth, paper and clay samples showing manipulation of materials.
Photo: Dan Bosworth.

thinking and suggest solutions which could then be brought into clay. Surfaces and forms can be re-created or reinvented in clay, assuming a kind of fossil-like permanence when fired. Found or made textures can be pressed into the clay and moulds could be made from certain objects. Clay can be worked in the same way as other materials, i.e. torn, cut and rolled, but will bring its own character to the pieces made.

Selecting from the following list of materials-handling descriptions may inspire you to make: you can rip, cut, bind, tear, fold, roll, link, tie, bolt, wrap, knot, plait, twist, weave, bundle, stitch, bend, pin, layer, pile, gather or cluster.

When these experiments are used to instigate design work, you will find you

Joy Bosworth, impressions in clay made by rope and fern. *Photo: Dan Bosworth.*

Emma Whitney, brooch, 2009. Porcelain fragment with layers of heat-coloured and patinated metal. 70 × 60 mm (2¾ × 2⅜ in.). *Photo: Dan Bosworth.*

are able to make body-adornment pieces which have a fresh look. Careful materials-handling skills, rather than the inherent value of the materials used, are what give these pieces their precious quality.

Emma Whitney, inspired by the natural decay and surface qualities on ancient buildings or unwanted objects, reproduces these surfaces in her beautiful objects. She has made the brooch above by bringing together layers of heat-coloured and patinated metal with a porcelain fragment. The wires which hold the piece together are attached to the porcelain fragment

with an electroplating technique, which leaves an encrustation of copper on the back and around the edge of the porcelain. She used this technique, which is more in keeping with the piece, as opposed to the more conventional ways of fabricating a bezel or a claw setting.

Ellen Ingram's stunning neckpiece (opposite) was inspired by the word 'cluster', and brings together many elements made from silver and porcelain, cleverly exploiting and contrasting the different qualities of the metal and porcelain.

Ellen Ingram, *Cluster neckpiece*, 2009. Porcelain with silver-plated copper and silver wire. Torque: 400 mm (15¾ in.), cluster: 140 × 100 mm (5½ × 4 in.). *Photo: Dan Bosworth.*

Chapter 2

Decorative clay surface techniques

Here are some techniques which work well for jewellery to get you started. More ideas can be found in other jewellery-making books (see bibliography).

Working with soft clay slabs

A number of different techniques to texture the surface, such as impressing stamps, rolling in a found texture, a mould taken from a found texture, and drawings scratched into a plaster block, can be used effectively for small jewellery pieces.

Impressing: Frank Fisher

Frank Fisher, the American artist and teacher, impresses old printing blocks into the surface of soft clay.

Handmade roulettes or stamps made from bisque-fired clay or plaster, such as those made by Sally and Alisdair

Frank Fisher, LEFT printing blocks used to make impressions in soft clay surfaces, 2008. RIGHT Earrings. *Photos: Frank Fisher.*

MacDonell, also work well. These surfaces can be used flat as medallions or brooches, rolled into a tube or pressed into a mould.

The picture sequence above shows the textured surfaces created with handmade stamps made from bisque-fired clay or plaster, showing how they are pressed into a plaster mould of a modelled face, which will become a brooch by Sally and Alisdair MacDonell.

1 Handmade bisque-fired clay and plaster stamps for making impressions.
2 Textured clay ready to be pressed into the mould of a face.
3 The press-moulded face with impressed patterns still showing.
4 Modelling additional details onto the face, which will be used as a brooch.
Photos: Dan Bosworth.

Steve Sedgwick, *Artefact with Rusty Metal*, 2008. 6 × 4.5 cm (2½ × 1¾ in.). *Photo: Dan Bosworth.*

Sprigs

A sprig is a pad of clay which has a pattern or detail, usually made in a small plaster mould, which is applied to a clay surface, giving a raised, textured area or relief. Sprigs are sometimes used in combination with impressed patterns, which are created in the opposite way (by pressing into the clay) and give a contrast to the sprig.

Steve Sedgwick's current jewellery pieces evolve from small test samples that he uses for decorating ceramic vessels. The original designs come from stamps and sprig-moulded patterns made on a thinly rolled slab. Steve was first drawn to motifs inspired by Asiatic bronzes, but he now uses a wide range of other designs as well as odd-shaped pieces of wood, metal and even gear wheels to produce a range of textured surfaces. He also makes stamps by carving or casting in plaster.

Sedgwick uses a matt yellow and a barium turquoise glaze that give a wide range of colours depending on how thickly they are applied and how much glaze is trapped by the surface texture. At first he only used the same mediumgrogged stoneware that he uses for making vessels, as this is very stable and gives a nice bronze body colour where glaze has been applied and wiped off. He now also uses Ashraf Hanna White Clay, which gives a more translucent quality to the glazes. Firing is at 1240°C (2264°F) in an electric kiln.

Rolling into a found texture

Found textures like lace, rubber matting or embossed wallpaper are ideal, as clay rolled onto these kinds of surface will very easily pick up the texture. Be aware, though, that if the found texture is non-absorbent, the clay may become stuck to the surface. It may be possible to get around this problem by carefully peeling away the found texture from the clay, or it may be that you should not press the clay too hard into the surface. A light dusting of flour onto the surface of the clay before pressing in the texture will help to separate the two, with any residue of flour burning off later in the kiln. Steve Sedgwick sprays a thin film of WD-40 to help release the clay from the found texture.

In the neckpiece by Kate Ibberson (see p.26), an old rubber hot water bottle was rolled into the surface of the clay. Then the clay was loosely folded and an additional flat piece was applied to the reverse to make it comfortable to wear. The holes were cut when the beads were leatherhard, so as not to damage the surface. The beads were then fired to stoneware temperature 1260°C (2300°F) with a cobalt barium glaze.

If the found texture is delicate or will perish with time, as, say, in the case of a savoy cabbage leaf, you can make a plaster mould from the leaf, so that the texture

A sample of found objects and the surface textures they create. *Photo: Dan Bosworth.*

can be picked up by a slab of clay being pressed into the surface of the mould.

Slip techniques

Using coloured slip can be very effective, and methods such as scraffito, combing, feathering, incising, marbling, inlaying and wax resist work well for small, flat jewellery pieces. These techniques can be found in more detail in other ceramic-making books, but here are a few examples.

Kate Ibberson, folded beads on silver torque, 2009. Stoneware-fired grey clay with cobalt barium glaze. Beads: 4 × 4 cm (1½ × 1½ in.), torque: 17 cm (6¾ in.). *Photo: Dan Bosworth.*

Carving a plaster block to create a raised design

This technique allows a fine, delicate line to be scored into the surface of a plaster block, which will form a raised decoration on the surface of soft clay pressed into it. This intricate design can be reproduced quickly once the plaster block has been made. A mirror image will be left in the clay surface, so any lettering needs to be scored in reverse.

Joanna Veevers paints coloured slips onto a plaster block into which she has scratched an intricate pattern. Then she creates a clay wall around the plaster slab and pours casting slip over it, which gives the thickness to the piece and picks up the detailed decoration.

Veevers shows in this series of images how she makes her intricate, patterned semi-porcelain brooches, sometimes using as many as five different coloured casting slips in one piece.

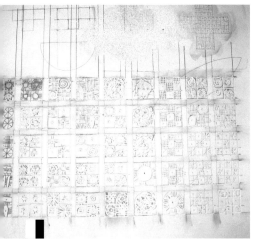

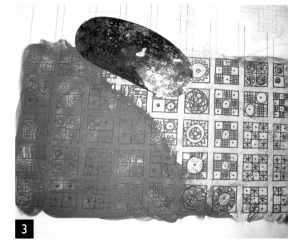

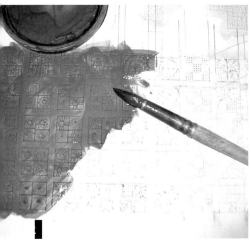

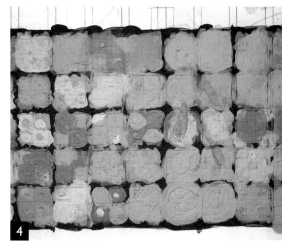

1 The design is drawn onto a smooth plaster block with a pencil and then scratched into the surface with a scalpel.

2 Black casting slip is painted over the surface.

3 When the slip has dried to leatherhard, the excess is scraped away with a metal kidney, leaving the design showing as black lines.

4 Different coloured casting slips are hand-painted into different areas.

5 A clay wall surrounds the block, and casting slip is flooded into the area.

Photos: Joanna Veevers.

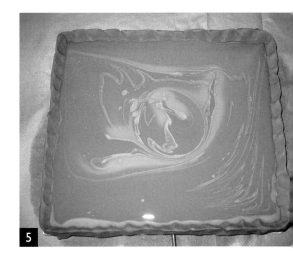

27

When the clay sheet is turned over the black slip delineates the colours. The finished pieces are cut into individual brooches. Each brooch measures approximately 40 × 25 mm (1½ × 1 in.). *Photo: Joanna Veevers.*

Inlaid slip

Marilza Gouvea carves the pattern directly into the surface of the red clay when leatherhard, and then paints on a thick layer of white slip. When this is dry (and wearing a mask to avoid the dust), Marilza scrapes off most of the white slip with a metal kidney tool, leaving an inlaid pattern.

Modelling onto the surface

Christy Keeney models onto the surface of flat brooches, which are made from a mixture of St Thomas Clay and Flax. This is similar to paper clay, giving strength when dry and minimizing shrinkage. He covers the brooches with an ivory earthenware slip. After a bisque firing, he paints the brooches with a mixture of 50% copper and 50% manganese dioxide, which is rubbed back to leave the dark lines and modelled areas. He then paints a small amount of coral red, blue and yellow underglazes to pull out details of the face and hair, covers the whole brooch with a fine wash of vanadium oxide, and fires to 1140°C (2084°F).

Burnishing

Burnishing or polishing the surface of clay that is beyond leatherhard and is almost dry gives a beautifully shiny surface that responds well to smoke or saggar firing. Kati Vamos has burnished this porcelain circular medallion (see p. 30), then used a resist method (as seen used by Jenny Crispin in the Firing chapter later in the book) with a saggar-firing technique to great effect.

Marilza Gouvea, neckpiece. Inlaid white slip on red clay with black rubber and silver. *Photo: Marilza Gouvea.*

Christy Keeney, *Suzi Brooch*, 2008. St Thomas and Flax clay with slip, oxides and underglazes fired to 1140°C (2084°F), 50 × 30 mm (2 × 1¼ in.). *Photo: Christy Keeney.*

Kati Vamos, *Medallion*, 2008, Thrown porcelain, burnished and saggar-fired. 50 mm (2 in.) diameter. *Photo: Kati Vamos.*

Chapter 3

Forming

Many of the making techniques already known to ceramic makers and written about in other ceramic books will be relevant for small-scale bead or jewellery work. For instance, handbuilding techniques such as slab work, the use of moulds, slipcasting, modelling and extruding are all relevant, and some ideas are suggested here.

Modelling

Aside from the hands, there are also a few tools that are useful in manipulating clay into forms. Sally and Alisdair MacDonell work together on the faces of their brooch forms. Sally models the faces as part of the process of making the original model for the plaster cast, then, to make each one more individual, Alisdair modifies them before casting and again after the clay face has been formed in the mould.

In this series of images (see p.32) Sally is modelling a face. She always makes an egg form from two pinch pots, as she likes to have the resistance of the air trapped inside the egg form whilst modelling. First she pushes two depressions for the eye sockets with her thumb; then she adds coils of clay tapering at each end for the eyes, nose and lips, with two balls of clay for the nostrils and a larger one for the chin. Tiny, modified wooden tools are used for detailed work to tidy up around the eyes, and a modified end from a ballpoint pen makes the irises. The

MacDonells like the faces to be slightly uneven so as to be more human and adult than doll-like. Plaster casts, usually done in batches, are then made from these faces. (See Chapter 2, p.23, for the way the plaster moulds are used with textured slabs of clay.)

Modelled beads

Plastic clay can be rolled in the palms of the hands either as irregular beads or by measuring exact quantities by cutting equal lengths from a coil of clay before rolling. This simple method can be very effective, as solid colours made with body stains can be used, without glaze, or otherwise various colours can be used together to create a marbled effect. The hand-rolled clay bead may then be rolled onto a texture.

You will need to make a hole in the bead, something that is better done when the clay has dried slightly so that the form is not distorted, although not too dry or the bead will crack. For larger holes a plastic drinking straw can be used, or else a proprietary hole-maker made of metal: both cut the hole cleanly, taking the unwanted plug of clay with them. For smaller holes a wooden cocktail stick or a piece of dry spaghetti work well, as both are absorbent and are less likely to stick to the clay as they are pushed through the bead. A burr of clay will be pushed through which you will need to remove with a sharp knife at the leatherhard stage.

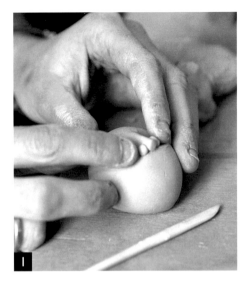

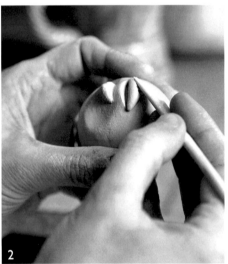

Sally MacDonell modelling a face.

1 Modelling the nose onto an egg form.
2 Modelling the lips.
3 Creating the chin.
4 Modelling the eyes.

Photos: Dan Bosworth.

Other, more sophisticated hole-makers are sold by pottery suppliers or kitchen shops; being hollow, these implements carry the plug of clay through the hole. Holes of different sizes and shapes, for function and decoration, can be made using these tools. Alisdair and Sally MacDonell have collected an impressive array of such tools from cookery shops and ceramic tool suppliers whilst on their travels.

Here Alisdair MacDonell makes a plaster mould of a face for a brooch that was modelled by Sally MacDonell.

1 The modelled face is placed onto a clay slab.
2 A clay wall surrounds the face.
3 Plaster of Paris is poured into the cavity.
Photos: Dan Bosworth.

Plaster of Paris moulds for handbuilding

Moulds are very useful to speed up the process of repeating forms. Plaster of Paris is cheap and can be bought from specialist suppliers in a dry state. As shown in the illustrations above, the Macdonells make plaster moulds for their brooches. Here the modelled face is attached to a slab of clay and surrounded by a cottle (clay wall). The plaster of Paris is then mixed as follows. Firstly, the volume of plaster needed is estimated by looking into the cavity created by the cottle (the surrounding clay wall) and estimating the amount of water needed to fill this space. Now half the estimated amount of water (the amount of water actually used is only half because the plaster expands in the water to fill the space within the cottle).

Pour the final amount of water into a large bowl or bucket. The Plaster of Paris is then sieved over the surface of the water until an island of plaster appears, whereupon one more handful of plaster is sprinkled around the outer edge of the water in the bucket. Leave the plaster and water for a couple of minutes until all the plaster has been soaked through, then gently agitate the mixture from the bottom until it becomes thicker, being careful not to introduce air into the mix. When the mixture begins to thicken, it can be poured into the prepared cavity. It is then gently pushed down to ensure that the plaster has been forced into every detail of the model and that air bubbles have been encouraged to the surface. If the estimated amount of plaster is not enough, then the surface should be roughened by dragging a finger through it as it is becoming solid, so that another mix can be made and poured over it. If too much plaster has been mixed then the excess should be poured into a rubbish bag, NOT down the sink, where it will block the drain hole.

How to make a two-piece mould for slipcasting

Slipcasting is a useful technique if a number of forms are to be made of the same shape. Here the making of a simple two-piece plaster mould is described.

The model to be cast can be made from clay or another material. If it is made from a non-clay material then a thin layer of Vaseline should be smeared over it before making the mould. The model is buried in clay to the point of undercut, which on a sphere would be the halfway point, but on a less regular shape would be the place where the form starts to change direction in such a way that the form to be cast would be trapped in the plaster if a join was not present. Once buried in plaster, any undercuts will prevent the piece from being pulled out. A chunky sausage of clay is set at right angles to the model to make a gully or opening for the slip to be poured into the mould. A wall, or cottle, made from clay, thick paper, plastic or rubber, is wrapped around the base of the item to create a cavity to hold the plaster. It is held in place with masking tape or string, with a rough sausage of clay pressed down around the base to make it waterproof.

The same process shown in the picture sequence (on p. 33) is used for making the first part of the two-piece mould. The mixed plaster is poured into the prepared area until it has a thickness of about 10 cm (4 in.) above the model.

When this has hardened, the cottle and clay are taken away, revealing the part of the model which was buried in clay, now held in the hardened plaster. This first part of the mould, which we will call part one, is rested on the board with the half-buried model facing upward. Natch marks, which are carved depressions of either angled or half-spherical shape, are cut into the plaster, to make it easier to position this part of the mould correctly onto part two (turning the edge of a small coin in the plaster makes a good natch hole). Soft soap (mouldmakers' size) is rubbed into the upper surface of the plaster and into the natch marks. This creates a barrier so that parts one and two do not stick together. A cottle is wrapped around part one, held in place with masking tape and sealed with a rough sausage of clay as before. Another mix of plaster is made and poured into the cottled area to

Catrin Mostyn Jones, Open mould for bangle. *Photo: Catrin Mostyn Jones.*

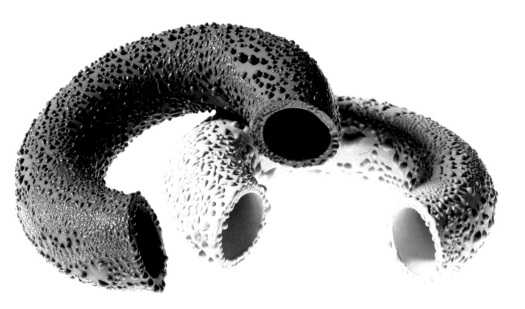

Catrin Mostyn Jones, *Bangles.* 2009. Slipcast, with underglaze colours and earthenware glazes. *Photo: Jenny Sadler.*

make part two of the mould. When this has hardened and the cottle is removed, the soft-soap barrier should have ensured that the two pieces of the mould will separate, and the model can be removed. The two parts of the mould will need to be completely dried before being used to slipcast. This can take a day or two, depending on temperature and humidity.

Catrin Mostyn Jones's two-piece mould (above, top) shows the natch marks and also the gully through which slip is poured in and out. Casting slip is a clay slip, made from water and deflocculant, which can be bought from ceramic suppliers. Soda ash and sodium silicate are deflocculants used in combination in a casting-slip recipe. It is possible to buy a manufactured combination of the two in liquid form (Dispex); this can be added to casting slip which has become too stiff, to loosen it or make it more liquid.

When used for slipcasting, the two parts of the mould are held together with rubber bands, masking tape or string; a sausage of clay seals the join, with another making a funnel around the mould's opening. The mould should be slightly overfilled with casting slip up into the clay funnel. As the mould begins to absorb the water from the slip that is touching the insides, the level of slip will decline and the mould may need to be refilled slightly. When the required thickness of casting slip has developed, the excess casting slip is poured out of the mould which is then left to drain and dry upside down. When the hollow clay object has dried to leatherhard it should be possible to release it from the two-piece mould. It is allowed to dry completely and the fine ridge of clay which shows at the point where the two parts of the mould join, may be fettled or shaved off with a scalpel or potter's knife. A mask should be used for the fettling process and the dry clay, which is fettled off, should be allowed to fall into a bowl of water. **Dry clay is hazardous if breathed in over a prolonged period.**

If the form is complicated then the plaster mould will need to be made in more than two pieces, and the separate parts of the mould will need to follow each point of undercut.

Catrin Mostyn Jones's colourful bangles (see p. 35) are slipcast using a two-piece mould made from a child's plastic toy, which, being smooth and even, is ideal, though a clay object or 'model' is just as easy to use. These bangles could also be extruded, a technique described later in this chapter.

Slab-building

Triangular rolled bead, Sue Crossfield

A technique used in paper-bead making, transferred to clay slabs by Sue Crossfield, is illustrated opposite.

1 An even slab of clay is rolled out and then textured with a roulette of fired clay.
2 Elongated triangles are then cut out of the textured clay.
3 After being brushed with a little water, the bead is rolled around a fine wooden dowel starting from the wider end.
4 The completed beads.
Photos: David Crossfield.

Textured, rolled tube bead, Sue Crossfield

Sue Crossfield textured the surface of the clay with a wooden butter pat and, after cutting it into rectangles, has carefully rolled the clay into a tube. The two edges are joined with a liberal coat of creamy slip before being gently pushed together around a former, with care taken not to damage the surface texture.

A The cut pieces are formed around a wooden dowel, and creamy slip is painted along the join.
B The finished beads.
Photos: David Crossfield.

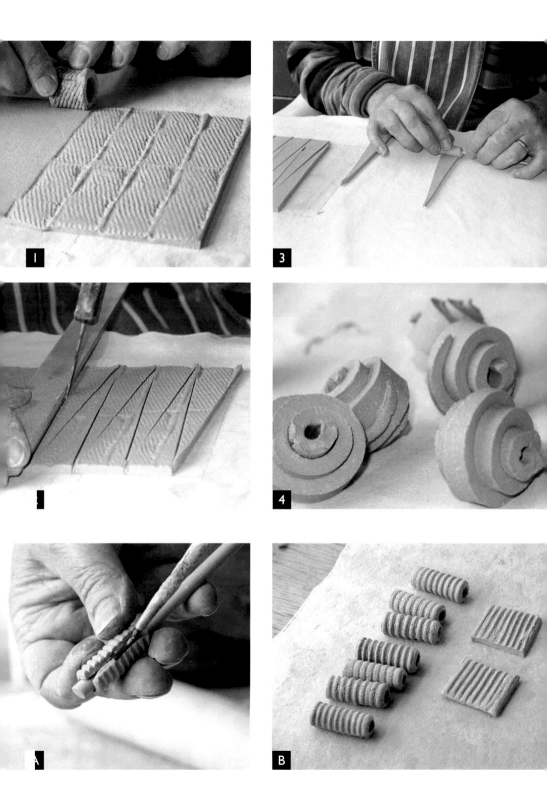

Throwing

Throwing on the potter's wheel, which is used by many potters as a quick way to produce vessels, is not the most obvious method for making jewellery components, but larger beads or tubes could be made in this way. Describing the techniques for throwing is not the subject of this book, as other pottery-technique books describe, in more detail, how one would go about learning to throw. Those who already know how to throw would find it more efficient to centre a large lump of clay then make the small beads or tubes from this lump called throwing 'off the hump'.

Joy Bosworth throwing small beads 'off the hump'. *Photo: Dan Bosworth.*

Extruding

Enticing forms can emerge very quickly from extruders, ideal for rapid production of large numbers of elements suitable for jewellery. Extruders can be large and wall-mounted, with many different die plates for many different shapes, both hollow and solid. They can also be table-mounted or handheld, rather like an icing pump.

Emma Whitney is interested in architecture and uses images taken during her travels in Europe to inspire her work. She has used extruded forms, cut and reassembled, to make architectural stands for her jewellery (see p.40). These become mini mixed-media sculptures when the jewellery is not being worn.

Extruded beads

A long hollow section can be made with a variety of bought or handmade dies (as seen opposite). These tube forms can be cut, bent or re-formed very quickly and easily. Blake and Janette Mackinnon made their *Black Pillow Beads* in this way (see p.40), fired to 1150°C (2102°F) with a hand-painted white opaque earthenware glaze, and re-fired to 780°C (1436°F) with platinum lustre. I also use extruded tubes, which I make into tubular beads by cutting them and decorating them by carving spiral marks. The photo on p.41 shows these unglazed, raku-fired, extruded beads, which are combined with dyed muslin to make neckpieces.

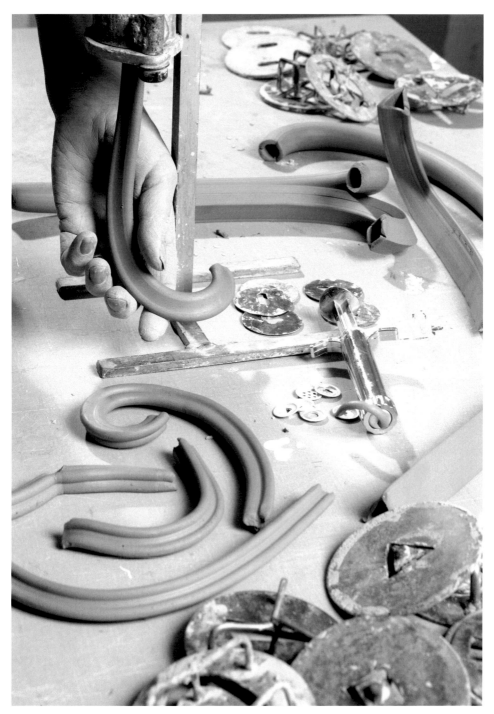

Extruders – tabletop and syringe-style – with extruder die plates and a range of possible extrusions. The largest of these fit a wall-mounted extruder. *Photo: Dan Bosworth.*

Emma Whitney, 2009. Copper and silver jewellery on extruded stoneware clay stands. *Photo: Graham Bradbury.*

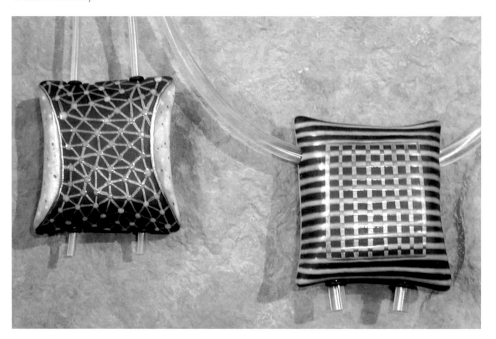

Blake and Janette Mackinnon, *Black Pillow Beads*, 2008. Extruded black Dorothy Fiebleman earthenware clay, fired to 1150°C (2102°F) with hand-painted white opaque earthenware glaze and platinum lustre re-fired to 780°C (1436°F). *Photo: Janette Mackinnon.*

Joy Bosworth, *Scarf Neckpiece*. Unglazed, raku-fired, extruded clay tubes with dyed muslin, l: 32 cm (12½ in.). *Photo: Dan Bosworth.*

Chapter 4

Colour

Ceramic jewellery components can be transformed by the use of colour, or by combinations of colours and other materials used in the finished piece. Colour in ceramics can be achieved through body stains, slips, glazes, lustres and enamels, as well as printing, firing techniques and the use of glass.

The American artist Sean Brown makes whimsical and colourful bird brooches that are further embellished with colourful feathers. Here a dyed peacock feather is used. Each piece is given its own personality by being hand-painted with glaze and with 22K gold lustre in a series of firings.

Body stains

These are manufactured colours and should be added to clay bodies at a rate of between 2 and 15% per 100% of clay, depending on the intensity of colour required. Body stains are a rather expensive way of adding colour to a piece, but jewellery is small and thus may be an economically viable use for this technique. There are several books

Sean Brown, *Whimsical Bird Brooch with Feather*, 2009. Earthenware glaze and 22K gold lustre, 38 × 29 mm (1½ × 1⅛ in.). *Photo: Sean Brown.*

Naomi Thompson, *Honesty Necklace* with drawings, 2008. Marbled porcelain with blue body stain and copper wire, l: 20 cm (8 in.), medallions: 9 mm (⅜ in.) diameter. *Photo: Dan Bosworth.*

which go into this in depth – Jo Connell's *Colouring Clay* is one (see bibliography).

Naomi Thompson has used the marbling technique for this neckpiece inspired by honesty seed heads. Porcelain has been coloured with body stain and then unevenly mixed into uncoloured porcelain, which gives a marbled effect as shown in the photo on p.43.

Body stain can also be used to colour slip, which could be used to decorate the surface of a piece as seen in the work of Joanna Veevers (see Chapter 2, p.27).

Glazes

Glaze will enhance the colour and texture, and in some cases may strengthen the piece. Makers of ceramics may have their own favourite glazes for use in jewellery. People just starting to make ceramic jewellery may wish to buy glazes from specialist suppliers. Some may wish to experiment with glazes using the jewellery pieces as a kind of 'test tile' for other work. Glaze must be wiped back from the surface that is touching the kiln shelf, or the piece needs to be suspended in the kiln, to stop the ceramic piece from sticking to the kiln shelf during firing. This is described in more detail in Chapter 5 on kilns and firing.

Stoneware glazes

A clay body fired to the point where it becomes vitrified in the temperature range 1250–1300°C (2282–2372°F) (most commonly these are buff and white clays) can be technically classed as stoneware. At this high temperature

Silver hand-formed and soldered ring by Astrid Harrison made from a stoneware reduction-fired celadon glaze droplet by Matthew Blakely. *Photo: Astrid Harrison.*

Rachel Wood, *Derbyshire Neckpiece* (detail), 2008. Lime-green barium stoneware glaze with hemp string. L: 55 mm (2⅛ in.). *Photo: Dan Bosworth.*

some colours are burned out (red and yellow are difficult, as are some pinks and purples). Typical colours tend to be autumnal browns, ochres, greens, blues and whites, although it is possible to achieve bright colours such as turquoise and shocking pink.

Matthew Blakely is known for his stoneware reduction-fired celadon glazes, which are designed to form droplets hanging from the lower edges of his bowls. Sometimes droplets fall onto the kiln shelf, and he has cleverly collaborated with Astrid Harrison, who has formed them into silver rings. Close study reveals bubbles trapped in the glaze.

Rachel Wood makes neckpieces inspired by the Derbyshire countryside, whose simplicity is enhanced by the complex surface she has perfected using a lime-green barium glaze over a vanadium slip, fired to 1260°C (2300°F).

Oxides

Oxides are used within the stoneware temperature range, with the main oxides being:

cobalt	blue
red iron	brown (green (celadon) in tiny quantities in reduction)
copper	green (pink in reduction)
manganese	brown-purple
tin	white
zirconium silicate	white
chrome	green (pink when combined with tin and lime, usually within a lead glaze at earthenware temps, but can also be achieved at stoneware temps)

Oxides are a natural colouring mineral which provide colour for stoneware glazes and can be applied directly to a bisque-fired piece. A small quantity of

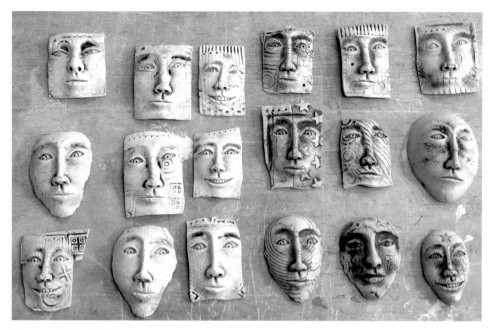

Sally and Alisdair MacDonell, *Face Brooches*, 2008. Nine awaiting glaze application and nine fired, finished with cobalt or copper oxide and a matt white stoneware glaze, 30 × 40 mm (1¼ × 1½ in.). *Photo: Dan Bosworth.*

the powdered oxide is added to water, which may then be painted or sponged onto the surface of a piece. It is particularly good for picking up texture, as any excess can be wiped back to leave oxide behind in the depressions of the texture.

Sally and Alisdair MacDonell enhance the details on their brooches (made using modelling and press-moulding techniques) with cobalt and copper oxide washed into the texture. In the above photo, a board of nine brooches awaiting the application of the matt white glaze, and then due to be fired to stoneware temperature (1260°C/2300°F), are shown next to nine brooches which have already been fired.

In the minimalist brooch by Susan Disley, shown opposite, white engobe was painted prior to the first firing, then copper carbonate painted around the edge and a line added. The copper carbonate has bled slightly into the white engobe, creating a halo effect.

Earthenware temperature glazes

Clay and glaze fired between 950°C and 1160°C (1742 and 2120°F) can be described as earthenware. Earthenware glazes are usually more shiny than stoneware (sometimes called bright) and have the ability to be more colourful. The clay is not as strong as clay fired to the higher stoneware temperature. The clay is still porous and the glaze sits on the top, often with fine cracks or crazes appearing on the surface.

Catrin Mostyn Jones's jewellery uses shocking colours taking inspiration from deep-sea creatures. This brooch (on p.47) contrasts the matt surface of purple

Susan Disley, untitled brooch, 2009. Stoneware, white engobe with copper oxide, 30 × 40 mm (1¼ × 1½ in.). *Photo: Svafa Einarsdottir.*

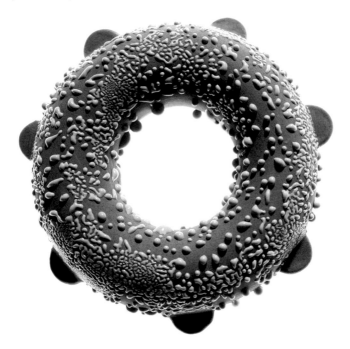

Catrin Mostyn Jones, *Portal Brooch*, 2008. Purple underglaze and blue earthenware glaze, dia: 60 mm (2⅜ in.). *Photo: Jenny Sadler.*

Blake and Janette Mackinnon, untitled neckpieces, 2008. Earthenware glazed cube beads, spheres and glass spacers. *Photo: Janette Mackinnon.*

underglaze with a rich blue shiny glaze that has drawn back into puddles because wax resist has been painted on the fired underglaze surface before the glaze is applied. The form has a bisque firing of 1120°C (2048°F), which is in the higher range for earthenware, making the pieces strong enough for jewellery.

Blake and Janette Mackinnon like the colourful glazes possible at earthenware temperatures, but to give more strength to the pieces, unusually, they bisque-fire

Ralf Dostmann, earthenware glazed beads. *Photo: Ralf Dostmann.*

to stoneware temperature (1250°C/ 2282°F) before firing their glazes at around (1040°C/1904°F) in a second firing, and then giving some a third lustre firing at (780°C/1436°F).

The image above shows a variety of brilliant earthenware coloured beads, fired to 1020°C (1868°F), made by Ralf Dostmann. He sells them as necklaces, but also independently so that they can be put together in different combinations for different effects.

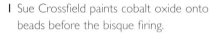

1 Sue Crossfield paints cobalt oxide onto beads before the bisque firing.
2 Sue Crossfield dips bisque-fired beads, threaded onto a knitting needle, into a barium stoneware glaze.
3 Sue Crossfield separates beads with a spatula as soon as they come out of the glaze, and allows them to dry before moving them.
Photos: David Crossfield.

Glaze application

Painting

Some manufacturers are making brush-on glazes in small quantities, which would be a good idea for those making ceramic jewellery. Three coats need to be applied with a soft brush to ensure that an even overall coating is made, but follow the manufacturer's instructions for best results.

Sue Crossfield paints cobalt oxide onto her beads, which she mixes with a little water to a painting consistency. She threads the dry beads onto a knitting needle whilst painting, so as not to get finger marks on the drying oxide. After a bisque firing, she is able to dip them into the stoneware glaze without the oxide contaminating the glaze in the bucket, while at the same time making sure that the hole in the bead does not become clogged up with glaze by using the knitting needle again.

Dipping

This is the quickest and most efficient way of applying an even overall layer of glaze without waste. It is important not to contaminate your glaze with oxides or other glazes which have previously been applied to the piece you want to dip. If you fear that it could be contaminated, you could decant a

Claire Ireland, *Leafy Pin*, 2008. Blue-grey stained, slipcast white earthenware; sponge-stamp wax-resist technique using mid-temperature red glaze, 20 × 20 mm (8 × 8 in.). *Photo: Claire Ireland.*

small amount of the glaze, but you must have enough depth to cover the piece. You may choose to dip only part of your piece or else to double-dip it in different glazes.

Sponging

Sponging is best done with a small natural sponge, which gives an uneven application to the glaze and allows for double application in some areas. This method of application gives an overall mottled effect that can be very attractive, picking up and enhancing textures.

Claire Ireland has made a decorative stamp out of a synthetic sponge by burning the design into the surface of the sponge with a soldering iron (a skewer heated in a gas flame would also do the job). The sponge stamp was used to print the design in water-soluble wax resist onto the bisque-fired pin, which was dipped into a mid-temperature earthenware red glaze and fired again.

Mervi Kervinen, *Las Palmas Geisha Balls*, 2008. Earthenware glaze with china-painting by Tranja Hasa, each sphere dia: 40 mm (1½ in.). *Photo: Kimmo Heikila.*

Pouring

Pouring may not be a suitable application method for small pieces, but for special effects on slightly larger pieces the runs that occur and the overlaying that is possible may give interesting effects.

Enamels and lustres

Enamels and lustres are especially effective for jewellery as they can give a precious quality, adding bright colourful and metallic highlights. They are fired to between 750 and 780°C (1382 and 1436°F) in a third firing, usually over a glaze, and remain on the surface. They are usually bought in tiny bottles mixed with pine oil or another carrying medium. **Note that lustres give off hazardous fumes and should always be used in a well-ventilated workshop with the kiln exhaust fumes extracted.**

The Finnish jeweler, Mervi Kervinen, works with jewel-like objects which she incorporates into videos. In the piece illustrated called *Las Palmas Geisha Balls*, she has made the geisha balls in a two-piece mould and, after glaze firing, has had them china-painted with enamels by Traja Hasa. They are joined together with a silver chain and worn entwined around the fingers.

Blake and Janette Mackinnon make a variety of beads in many different colours, styles and forms. The spherical beads in the image (opposite, top) fired to 1250°C (2282°F) at bisque, are then painted with blue underglaze with a transparent glaze applied over, fired to 1040°C (1904°F), and then put into a third lustre firing, with platinum and gold lustre, to 780°C (1436°F).

ABOVE Blake and Janette Mackinnon, blue and white beads with gold and platinum lustre. *Photo: Janette Mackinnon.*

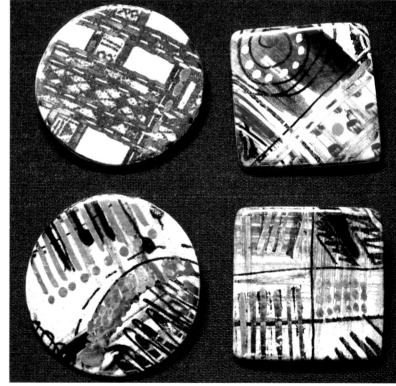

RIGHT Pollie and Garry Uttley, brooches, 2008. Painted, monoprinted, fired with earthenware glaze and lustre, 40 × 25 mm (1½ × 1 in.). *Photo: Garry Uttley.*

Virginia Graham, brooches on display cards, 2008. Coloured slips, underglazes and enamel transfers. *Photo: Toril Brancher.*

Printing

Pollie and Garry Uttley's work is inspired by Indian textiles; their brooches combine painting, monoprinting, glazing and hand-painted lustres. First, diluted underglaze colour is applied directly onto the plastic clay to give a painterly effect, then, when this has partially dried, a monoprint is transferred to the surface using black underglaze colour. The pieces are fired first to 1080°C (1976°F) with a honey or grey glaze, then for a second time to 750–780°C (1382–1436°F) with the further embellishment of gold or silver lustres.

Virginia Graham's colourful brooches are coloured with slips and underglazes under a transparent stoneware glaze. She fires on the manufactured enamel transfers in a third firing to 830°C (1526°F), as the colours are richer at this temperature.

Egyptian paste

Egyptian paste is the oldest form of glazed ceramic material. Made from a combination of clay, glaze and soluble sodium salts, it behaves like putty and is difficult to manipulate into anything but small amulets or beads. When drying, the glaze materials rise to the surface, with the soluble sodium salts producing crystals. Egyptian paste objects are once-fired when the surface crystals melt, which becomes the glaze. Being low-fired, the components made from Egyptian paste will not be strong and so should be small and preferably of a strong form such as a spherical bead or thicker flat form.

Isabel Denyer uses Egyptian paste beads together with beads made from precious metal, clay and porcelain. Some makers who use Egyptian paste measure out the ingredients dry, putting them into a plastic bag so that they can be manipulated, to mix them, from the outside of the bag. Only when the Egyptian paste is needed, is the water added to the plastic bag. Manipulating the mixture from the outside of the bag is a tidy way of working that saves the hands from the drying properties of the soda ash. So long as the dry ingredients are mixed well inside the plastic bag, small quantities for immediate use can be decanted into another plastic bag and mixed with the water. Fire to 900 or 910°C (1652 or 1670°F) for a slightly stronger colour.

Melted glass surfaces

Window or picture glass softens at around 800°C (1472°F) and melts at 1060°C (1940°F), but these temperatures may vary depending on the size of granules and the type and thickness of glass used. Glass will withstand stoneware temperatures but needs to be contained within a well or within deep textures to stop it spilling over onto the kiln shelf. It will crack upon cooling, giving a crazed pool that, surprisingly, has a smooth surface and can be used as a decorative device. Coloured bottle glass can also be used but may be more prone to faults such as bubbling or scumming (the appearance of a white powdery layer of devitrified glass).

Oxides and/or glazes can be used with

Isabel Denyer, Egyptian paste, porcelain and precious-metal clay beads, l: 48 mm (1⅞ in.). *Photo: Isabel Denyer.*

Margaret Smith and Joy Bosworth, neckpiece, 2008. Porcelain with melted glass, glass beads, silver and copper, l: 48 mm (1⅞ in.) *Photo: Dan Bosworth.*

the glass to give colour, and copper or cobalt oxides are also very effective, giving a beautiful turquoise or blue respectively. It is always best to test glass first before using it on a finished piece.

It is possible to buy powdered glass from specialist suppliers, and crushed bottle or scrap picture glass can also be used. If you need to crush the glass into smaller pieces then you should wrap it in ten or so layers of newspaper, place the newspaper bundle on the floor and then hammer it. Goggles should be worn when you do this. Hammered

glass fragments can vary from as large as 4mm (¼ in.) to as small as dust particles, but if too much glass dust is used then the glass is more likely to bubble as air will become trapped in the molten glass.

Margaret Smith's porcelain medallion fired to 1260°C (2300°F), with melted, crushed bottle glass, has been made into a pendant with a copper claw setting, added to a three-strand necklace made by Joy Bosworth from glass and copper-tube beads (see photo above).

Chapter 5

Firings and kilns

Small electric kilns

Anyone buying their first kiln will find an electric kiln is the easiest to manage. These days, ceramic fibre is often used in the construction of electric kilns, making them lighter, cheaper to buy and more fuel-efficient.

The life of kiln elements depends on the temperature to which they are fired and the frequency of firing. Electric kiln elements will darken as they age and small dark spots or blemishes occur; they also become brittle and may sag out of the grooves that house them. It is best to replace all elements together, as old elements will become strained when fired with new elements, and will fail more quickly.

As a jeweller, if you're going to buy a small electric kiln, you might consider an enamel kiln, on account of its cheapness, its speed at reaching temperature, and the prospect of being able to use it for metal enamelling. The door is easy to open but should not be opened whilst the kiln is hot as it is likely to damage the electric kiln elements; however, there is usually a window in the door so that you can see what is happening inside the kiln. The downside would be its lack of capacity to be fired slowly enough for bisque, and also that its absolute maximum temperature would be 1000°C (1832°F), limiting it to the low earthenware temperature range. It is possible to use enamel kilns in conjunction with a temperature indicator and regulator which shows the temperature and firing details during firing, and controls the firing process electronically.

A test kiln is considerably more expensive and is designed to have a firing cycle programmed into an electronic controller. This kiln can fire to stoneware temperatures (up to 1300°C/2372°F) and, as such, is everything that a larger modern electric kiln should be, except for its size. It can be used just like any sophisticated electric kiln, being able to perform bisque and glaze firings up to stoneware and porcelain temperatures.

If you plan to spend the equivalent of what it would take to buy a test kiln, it may be better to buy the smallest top-loader, like the Potterycrafts Mercury Plug and Go electric top-loader P5922/SP (see p.58), for example. Capable of being fired up to 1300°C (2372°F), it can be programmed with either a single or a multi-phase digital controller.

Blake and Janette MacKinnon use a small test kiln which Blake made himself, and which can be packed efficiently to fire a large number of beads at the same time. For glaze firing, they use tile cranks which they have modified for use as bead racks. Tile cranks are a set of supports which allow tiles to be stacked up in order to use the kiln space economically. These have been adapted with nichrome wire threaded through to

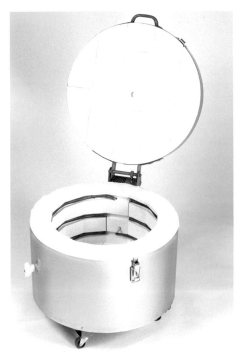

Potterycrafts Mercury Plug and Go small electric top-loader. *Photo by permission of Potterycrafts.*

Blake and Janette Mackinnon's small electric kiln packed with beads. *Photo: Janette Mackinnon.*

support the beads so that they do not touch each other.

Small gas kiln

A small top-hat kiln could be made relatively cheaply using wire mesh and ceramic-fibre blanket, and fired with a gas torch and propane gas bottles. The kiln's small scale means that wire mesh that can be bought from building suppliers or garden centres would be suitable. Once cut into the sizes required, the mesh is bent into a cylinder and held in place by Kanthal wire (known also as Nichrome wire), which is heat-resistant and is thus used to make kiln elements. The lid of the kiln is cut from the mesh, bent, and held in place with the Kanthal wire. Two holes are made, one in the middle of the top to act as a chimney hole, and the other at the bottom of the side wall to take the gas torch. Aluminium foil is used to line the inside of the mesh structure, and the ceramic blanket is cut to shape and pushed into place against the aluminium foil. Stoneware-fired buttons or ceramic board squares, tied into position with Kanthal wire, hold the ceramic blanket in place.

The top-hat kiln rests on a square of wire mesh, aluminium foil and ceramic blanket. The surface of the blanket that is exposed to the heat is sprayed with a rigidiser, which hardens and protects the surface. It is best to work out of doors when making the kiln and to wear a mask to protect yourself from

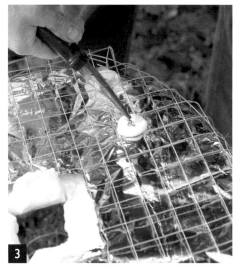

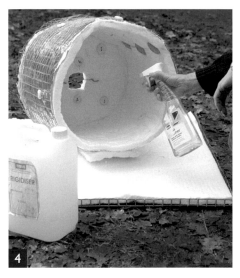

loose fibres that might be released from the ceramic blanket.

Kiln furniture which is made for test kilns can be used in conjunction with this kiln.

A single gas torch should be enough for such a small kiln, and if it is put through a hole in the bottom of the kiln's side, at an angle, then the heat will radiate around the kiln, spiralling up and through the hole in the top. A small

Photo sequence for the small top-hat kiln:

1 The wire mesh shell of the kiln being bent and fastened with Nichrome wire.
2 The hole cut for the chimney.
3 Ceramic fibre held in place with ceramic buttons inside and out, and Nichrome wire.
4 Spraying the inside of the kiln with rigidiser.
Photos: Dan Bosworth.

CONTINUES OVERLEAF

5

6

5 The kiln with the propane gas torch in position.

6 A portable digital temperature indicator put in place through a hole in the kiln side.

Photos: Dan Bosworth.

mesh cylinder lined with ceramic blanket could make a removable chimney that would aid the flow of air and the rise in temperature, especially for stoneware firings.

A further asset would be a portable digital temperature indicator, enabling you to observe the exact temperature inside; otherwise the temperature will need to be gauged by the use of pyrometric cones or by looking at the colour inside the kiln and the state of the glaze melt. A kiln like this would need to be closely monitored and the temperature controlled by opening the valve on the burner as the temperature rises. It should be possible to achieve stoneware temperatures in this kiln.

Bonfire and smoke firing

Firing beads and small pieces in a simple bonfire kiln may be an exciting introduction for the beginner. Beads and smaller pieces of jewellery do not necessarily have to be bisque-fired prior to smoke firing. If a still, warm day is chosen and the kiln is left to cool naturally, then the firing will probably be successful. The ceramic pieces will only be fired to 600°C (1112°F) using this method, and will achieve a palette ranging from muted greys and browns through to black.

The simplest way of building this kind of kiln would be to dig a hole, line it with combustible materials – wood, brushwood, straw, wood shavings, dry leaves and paper – and place into it the beads and small ceramic pieces. The beads can be threaded onto Nichrome wire so that they do not become lost in the ash. Brushwood and larger pieces of wood are laid over the ceramic work along

Bead with crank resist layer. *Photo: Jenny Crispin.*

Metal smoke-firing chamber with incinerator lid, shown during firing. *Photo: Dan Bosworth.*

with straw and other combustible materials. The fire will burn for a number of hours until the required colour is achieved. When the fire is completely out and the ceramic pieces are cold, they can be rescued from the ashes and washed. Experiments will afford you some element of control as you learn what works and what does not. Chemicals such as copper sulphate and iron chromate, mixed with water and sprayed or painted onto some areas of the pieces together with copper carbonate and salt sprinkled in and around the beads, will give colours from yellow through to pinks and rusts. (Several books offer more in-depth information on bonfire and pit-firings such as *Smoke-fired Pottery* and *Low Firing and Burnishing,* see Bibliography.)

Jenny Crispin and Karen Warner use a similar technique to the one described above, but they use a metal container with an incinerator lid, into which they place wood shavings with the ceramic beads. They light from the top and allow the fire to burn through. They have collaborated in this way to make a simple but effective necklace. The spherical bead was smoke-fired with resist marks then polished. By combining it with simple bought findings they have made a distinctive piece (see p.62).

Tessa Wolfe Murray developed her smoke-firing technique as a result of determined necessity coupled with a fascination with fire. She did not want to conform to the usual smoke-firing technique of burying the pieces in sawdust, which smoulders for between 8 and 24 hours, as she wanted to glaze the inside of her pots and to have more control over the smoking process.

Before the smoking process, the vessel forms are relatively high-fired, with glaze where necessary, for strength and function. She works outside, smoking in a shallow metal meat tin. She found that she could heat the pieces to 100°C (212°F), and then sawdust soaked in

ABOVE Jenny Crispin and Karen Warner, Finished bead mounted with fluorite and Bali silver beads on a silver torque, 2008. L: 50 mm (2 in.). *Photo: Jenny Crispin.*

ABOVE RIGHT Tessa Wolfe Murray smoke-firing. *Photo: Anna Thorell.*

RIGHT Smoke-fired jewellery by Tessa Wolf Murray. *Photo: Anna Thorell.*

white spirit was sprinkled on the selected area. The instant fire that resulted caused the surface to be permanently affected by the carbon. She also found that it was possible to mask off some areas with damp sawdust. She says that this surface quality is permanent and could only be lost if it was to be re-fired to 600°C (1112°F) in an oxidising atmosphere. This technique was developed for her vessel forms, but she now also uses it for her jewellery.

Micro- and mini-kilns for use in a microwave oven

A relatively new kiln, made by an American company, Spectrum Kilns, which fires to 900°C (1652°F) in three minutes inside a normal 1200-watt home microwave, may be of interest for small-scale jewellery makers. It is made in two sizes: micro-kiln (internally), dia: 70 mm (2³/₄ in.), ht: 40 mm (1¹/₂in.); mini-kiln (internally), dia: 110 mm (4³/₈ in.), ht: 45 mm (1³/₄ in.). (See the list of suppliers at the end of the book for the UK distributor). Amazingly, it is possible to use glass, ceramic or metal pieces inside this kiln, inside the micro-wave. The manufacturers sell coloured multipens of glaze for use with these miniature kilns in 18 different colours;

these are lead-free, intermixable and dishwasher-proof.

One drawback of these kilns when used with ceramics is that only bisque ware can be put into them, so access to another kiln is necessary to do the initial bisque firing. Also, because of its small size, only one or two pieces at a time can be fired. Its possible advantages are its cheapness, and its speed and ease of use within the home even for those with little experience. Great care should be taken, as the inside of the kiln gets up to 900°C (1652°F), far greater than a normal oven. Moreover, although the kiln is very well insulated, the outside still gets hot, so insulated gloves should be worn and a heatproof surface should be used when retrieving it from the microwave oven. It goes without saying that the kiln should only be used by adults in a carefully controlled environment.

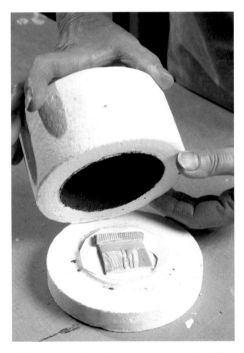

A Spectrum micro-kiln ready to be placed in a microwave oven. *Photo: Dan Bosworth.*

Firing guide for a 1200 watt microwave

micro-kiln		
copper	*ceramic*	*glass*
3 mins	3 mins 30 secs	4 mins
mini-kiln		
copper	*ceramic*	*glass*
8 mins	10 mins	10 mins

Packing jewellery in kilns

Obviously, it would be more cost-effective for ceramic makers to put jewellery pieces in and around other larger pieces in the bisque firing. For glaze firings, any unglazed or flat pieces can be put under and around pots and larger pieces. However, if glaze is present then it must not be allowed to touch the kiln shelves; thus glaze should be wiped away from any area which will touch the kiln shelf, or the pieces should be held away from the kiln shelf on some sort of rack. Bead racks are sold for this purpose, but you need to check that the rods which come with the rack will withstand stoneware temperatures, as there are certainly some on sale that will only withstand 1240°C (2264°F).

Beads which have holes can be threaded onto short lengths of Kanthal (also known as Nichrome) wire and slung between kiln props. Although it can withstand the stoneware temperatures, the wire will sag slightly and could allow beads to bunch together and stick to each other, so it is best to use short lengths with only one or two beads. Alternatively, the bisque-firing could be taken to stoneware temperature for strength, then fired to a lower earthenware temperature for the glaze, allowing for brighter colours. Because the Kanthal wire does not sag at

Isabel Denyer, beads on a bead rack. *Photo: Isabel Denyer.*

earthenware temperatures there is no worry of the beads sticking together during the glaze firing.

Another way of placing beads into the kiln is to make a stoneware tray with depressions that will stop beads from rolling about when they are placed in the kiln. The beads should have one surface wiped back so that no glaze touches the tray. If the bead is part-glazed, you could apply coloured slip to the unglazed surface whilst the clay is still malleable. Alternatively, the bead could be fired to stoneware temperature with a stoneware glaze applied to half of its surface, then re-fired standing on the stoneware-fired glaze half (which will not melt when fired to an earthenware temperature) with a low-temperature glaze. The disadvantages of this method are that glaze may run onto the kiln shelf if applied too thickly, and as the beads are re-fired it is less efficient in terms of energy and time needed to process them.

Chapter 6

Some simple metal techniques

Some ceramicists may prefer to work with a jeweller for more complex pieces, but if you can learn basic metalworking techniques, then your ideas for jewellery-making using ceramics will progress into a different sphere. The tools shown opposite are reasonably priced and can be bought a few at a time, when needed.

Sawing

For jewellery-making, a piercing saw is used which allows complex shapes to be cut and produces a clean, sawn edge that is easily filed. If tin snips are used to cut out the shape, the edge will be damaged, meaning a lot of extra time is needed to file and clean up the piece. A piercing saw consists of a frame, which if possible, should be adjustable so as to enable different-sized pieces of metal to be sawn. The fine blades, which are easily broken, are held in place by two wing nuts. The serrated edge of the blade should face away from the frame, and the serrations should point downhill, rather like a child's drawing of a Christmas tree. The blade should be inserted whilst pushing against the frame so that, once in place, it has a springy tension.

The sheet of silver or other metal to be sawn is laid flat onto the jeweller's peg.

The piercing-saw frame is always held in an upright position, with the blade allowed to stroke the metal without pressure being applied, as pressure will break the blade. By sliding the blade gently up and down, you let the serrated edge do the sawing, leaving the wrist free to alter the direction of the saw frame, thus allowing intricate shapes to be sawn (see image 1 in the series of photos describing how to make a bracelet, on p.71).

Bending

Silver and copper are soft metals which in the form of thinner sheets or finer wires can be bent between the fingers. Pliers or templates are needed to control the shape to be bent, though triblets, anvils, leather sandbags and other formers can be used, along with wooden or plastic mallets or hammers. When metal is worked either by bending or forming, it becomes work-hardened after

RIGHT Tools for forming soft metals such as gold, silver, brass or copper: a piercing saw, round-nose pliers, a plastic mallet, a general-purpose or ball-plein hammer, a hand drill, a file, a scribe, needle files, square-nose pliers, two types of wire cutters, a portable jeweller's peg and block. *Photo: Dan Bosworth.*

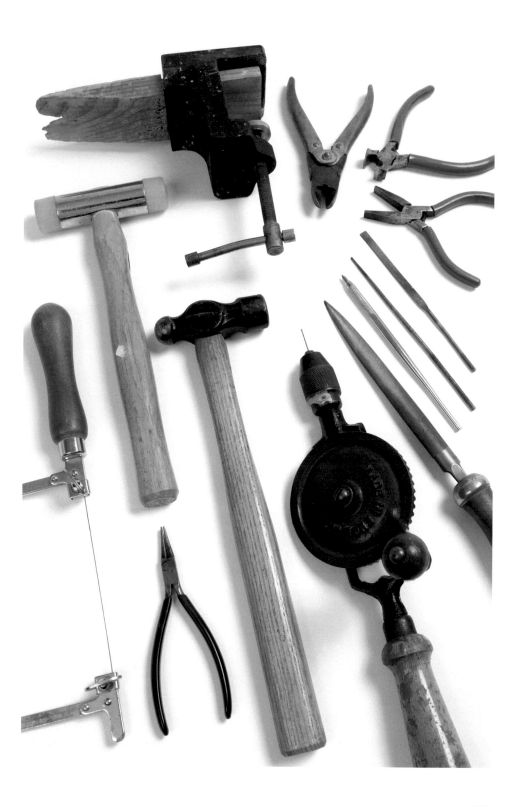

a time, and the tension in the metal can be felt as it stiffens. To soften the metal again it is necessary to anneal it.

Annealing and cleaning

Annealing means that the metal is heated with a gas torch. In the case of silver, gold, copper or brass, when the metal has melted to cherry-red colour, it has reached the temperature needed to anneal the metal. The temperature causes the surface to be oxidised, making it necessary to clean the surface in diluted acid, known as 'pickle'. **Pickle is an acidic solution that can be made from diluted sulphuric acid in the ratio of ten parts water to one part sulphuric acid. You should always add the acid to the water rather than the water to the acid.**

Pickle works more effectively if heated gently in an unbreakable glass or stainless-steel vessel inside a water-filled saucepan; do not allow it to become too hot.

Safe pickle crystals can be bought from specialist suppliers. Some safe pickles are made from already-diluted sulphuric acid and some are made from alum, a more pleasant substance. To make up the pickle solution dissolve a small amount of the crystals in a small amount of water, following the manufacturer's instructions. Only use brass or copper tweezers to retrieve work from the pickle solution, as steel tweezers will damage the pickle, causing a pink hue to attach itself to the jewellery being cleaned.

Soldering

Soldering is a term used for the process where two pieces of metal are joined together with heat, flux and solder. The following four sections describe the process, and the photos on pp.71–3 show how it is used to make a piece of jewellery.

Jewellers' torches

The torch shown in the photo on p.69 is relatively cheap and very portable, fuelled by lighter gas. It will only solder joints on little pieces like jump rings, but with its small flame it is ideal for findings because the flame is easy to direct onto a particular spot. For larger pieces you will need a larger jeweller's torch, of the kind sold by jewellery suppliers, with a variety of heads for different sizes of jobs. Potters may have a torch for drying out clay when throwing or for portable raku kilns, but, unless a jeweller's head can be fitted, you will not be able to use it.

NB When two pieces are to be joined together with solder, they need to be clean, to have a flux and to have the solder in place. When heated, the two pieces of metal need to reach the same temperature at the same time for the solder to flow. If it doesn't flow when heated, one or more of these requirements have not been met and you will need to clean the piece and set up again.

Fluxes and solder

Borax flux cones are bought from specialist suppliers and used with a borax dish. The cone is ground against the dish

RIGHT Soldering tools: (from top left clockwise) solder paste, tin snips, easy solder, borax flux, a small torch, iron binding wire, soldering tongs, brass tweezers, a brush. *Photo: Dan Bosworth.*

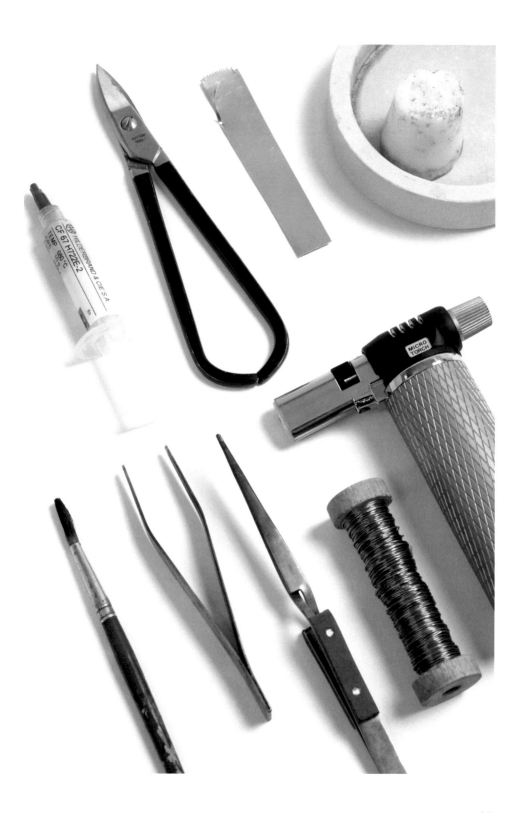

69

with a little water until a milky solution is achieved. This solution is brushed onto the joint and the pallions (small squares) of silver solder, ensuring that everything remains clean during the soldering process and encouraging the flow of solder. The tiny pallions of silver solder are cut into the flux dish and transferred with the flux brush or tweezers onto the joint. Solder comes in gold or silver and is made in three different types – hard, medium and easy – to melt at three different temperatures. When three different consecutive soldered joints are necessary, the hard solder is used for the first joint, the medium for the second and the easy for the third. Obviously, one would not want the first solder to melt and come apart when soldering the following joints.

The flux solution is painted directly onto the joint, and the pallions of silver solder are positioned at the point of the joint. The area is heated to melt the solder first into a ball, then into the joint. (See the making of the *Button Ring* on pp.73–4.)

Soldering paste is more expensive but is easier than silver solder pallions to position on the joint to be soldered. It consists of silver solder powder and flux, presented as a paste held in a syringe, and it stays in the position it is placed because of its paste-like consistency. It is used with a borax flux as before, painted onto the surface of the joint.

Cleaning solutions

You need to 'pickle' or clean a piece between each joint to be soldered and at the end of soldering, so as to remove the oxidised surface on the metal as well as any excess flux, which leaves a glass-like residue on the surface. It is possible to buy safety pickle in crystal form from jewellery suppliers. Two heaped teaspoons of safety pickle are added to about half a litre of cold water, and this solution is heated on a hob inside a heatproof container sitting in a saucepan of water. The solution should not be boiled but works more quickly when gently heated. Brass tweezers should always be used to retrieve pieces from the pickle, because steel tools will contaminate the solution, causing any copper that may be present in the pickle to cling to the surface of any silver or gold submerged in it.

Polishing

Once a piece has been completed and pickled, you will usually need to polish it. If you don't have a polisher (a soft rotating brush used with jeweller's rouge), then a metal-cleaning solution bought from a hardware shop and rubbed in with a soft cloth will do the job. You will also need to wash the piece in warm water with a drop of washing-up liquid before drying.

Jeweller's pendant motor

Those who become very interested in the metalwork side of the jewellery-making may find a jeweller's pendant motor to be a useful purchase. You can buy many different heads for the motor, to make all sorts of jobs – drilling, grinding, abrading and polishing – both quicker and easier to accomplish. It is hung directly above the jeweller's peg (work table). When a polishing mop is used in conjunction with the pendant motor, jeweller's rouge – a red, slightly abrasive wax polish – is applied to the mop before polishing to aid the process. Once this is finished, any residue of the rouge is

washed off with hot water and a mild detergent.

In the series of images above of the making of an *Elliptical Bracelet*, it can be seen how, with simple metalwork techniques, a slightly more advanced bracelet may be made, and how the idea could be further developed into a matching medallion, as seen on p.72.

Basic techniques of sawing, bending and a more advanced use of soldering

The making of an *Elliptical Bracelet*, by Joy Bosworth:

1 The silver rod, having been bent by hand, is cut with a piercing saw.
2 The two pieces are brought together before soldering.
3 The joints are soldered after the bead, with its outsized jump ring, is threaded on.
4 The joints are refined ready for polishing.
Photos: Dan Bosworth.

71

The finished *Elliptical Bracelet* with matching neckpiece. Joy Bosworth, 2008. Silver rod, silver wire and raku-fired bead, 80 × 50 mm (3⅛ × 2 in.). *Photo: Dan Bosworth.*

can be brought together to make a more complex piece, as seen above and on p.74, using a button made by Dawn Michelle van Gerven. Silver rod is bent around a former to make the ring shape, which is soldered (see images 2 and 3).

The problems encountered in this piece occur when two parts are brought together for soldering. When the two pieces of metal are of different sizes or thicknesses, the torch needs

Joy Bosworth making a ring, using a ceramic button by Dawn Michelle van Gerven.

1 Using a piercing saw to cut the silver shape.
2 Holding the ring in soldering tweezers for soldering, just as the solder melts into a ball.
3 Solder has melted and run into the join.
4 Drill two holes to correspond with two diagonal holes in the button.

Photos: Dan Bosworth.

CONTINUES OVERLEAF

5 The two pieces of the ring are brought together with medium solder when both have reached the same temperature.

6 Two wires are soldered into the holes in the circular plate.

7 The button is positioned using two-part epoxy glue, and the wires brought over with round-nose pliers, turning them into 'threads'.

Photos: Dan Bosworth.

to be played more over the larger or thicker piece to start the heating process before it is played over both parts. This was particularly difficult when soldering the two wires, which are very fine. The solution was not to play the torch directly onto the wires, but to let them pick up residual heat from the flame. Hard, medium and easy solder were used for the three separate solder joints.

Rivets

A rivet is a rod or tube of metal placed through a hole in two or more layers of material, both ends of which are spread with a punch and hammer to hold the layers firmly together. In the image on p.75 the square ring has a handmade decorative rivet in the centre as a design feature. It is possible with a soft metal to gently bend over the rivet quadrants

Two rings, 2008: a printed stoneware-fired button with four holes by Dawn Michelle van Gerven, made into a silver and ceramic ring by Joy Bosworth; and a glazed stoneware button with a handmade silver rivet in the centre, made by Joy Bosworth. *Photo: Dan Bosworth.*

with round-nose pliers without cracking the ceramic element whilst holding things in position. However, it is not advisable to use the conventional rivets normally used by jewellers, as the pressure needed to spread the metal that holds the two elements in place would crack the ceramic element.

Chloe Doran has used found objects from her uncle's workshop and other recycled materials in her *Memory Brooch*, seen on p.76. She has been able to use rivets to join the two pieces of metal together but has chosen to attach the ceramic element with a length of dyed jute yarn.

More advanced techniques

Chris Hay has formed the brooch on p.76 from stainless-steel balls laser-welded together around a ceramic shape without damaging the ceramic component. A laser welder is a very sophisticated piece of equipment, and very useful in some cases, as it produces a fine pinpoint of extreme heat which melts two metals together without solder and does not heat-affect the remainder of the piece.

Maddie Harris's dramatic *Bolivia Ring* (p.78) was made as a reaction to her surroundings on a number of different trips abroad, but mainly in response to her time in Bolivia. She was struck by the huge contrasts of wealth and poverty

Chloe Doran, *Memory Brooch*, 2009. Reassembled found metal elements with rivets, ceramic bead and dyed jute yarn, 40 × 30 mm (1½ × 1⅛ in.). *Photo: Dan Bosworth.*

Chris Hay, Untitled brooch, 2009. Stoneware clay and laser-welded stainless steel balls, 40 × 20 mm (1½ × ¾ in.). *Photo: Dan Bosworth.*

Bonnie Styles and Joy Bosworth, *Lace Necklace*, 2009. Electroplated ceramic lace with pearls and silver fastenings. *Photo: Dan Bosworth.*

Maddie Harris, *Bolivia Ring*, 2009. Formed and soldered copper and smoke-fired crank-clay ring, 50 × 20 × 20 mm (2 × ¾ × ¾ in.). *Photo: Dan Bosworth.*

and how things like newly introduced electricity generators made such a difference to the crumbling village buildings. In this ring (above) she suggests these contrasts by using the very different properties of copper with an extruded, smoke-fired crank-clay element. The copper sheet was cut using a piercing saw and was soldered together in separate sessions with hard, medium and easy solder. The crank-clay extruded tube is held together with two strips of copper sheet soldered to the base of the ring and folded back against the extruded tube.

Bonnie Styles collects antique lace and is continually researching how it can be brought into her jewellery pieces. In the necklace on p.77 she has selected a piece of antique lace from her collection, which has been soaked in porcelain slip and fired to 1260°C (2300°F) before being electroplated with silver. Electro-plating is a complex procedure, so she has this part of the process done by a small specialist company.

Chapter 7

Findings

Findings make a piece of jewellery function properly, and thus should always be an important consideration when designing. Findings are the mechanics of a piece – cords, chains, hooks, jump rings, brooch backs, earring wires and fastenings – and they can be bought readymade from specialist suppliers either by mail order, or at craft or hobby shops, or by visiting jewellery or bead fairs.

The right findings complete a piece in a quick, efficient and tidy manner. Considerations as to how the piece will work – whether it will be rigid or move with the wearer – are fundamental, and should be part of the initial process in which the style or theme of the jewellery or body adornment to be made is decided. As mentioned in Chapter 1 on designing, visual research is helpful, as ideas for different findings can be seen in museums, shops and galleries. However, it is also possible and certainly quicker to research on the internet for specific findings or to obtain a catalogue from the supplier that will give you photographs as well as names, sizes and prices of different findings.

Manufactured metal findings

Metal findings that can be bought cheaply in craft and hobby shops will probably be made from base metal. For a more durable and professional quality it is better to use findings made from precious metals like solid silver or gold, or silver- or gold-plated metal, which need to be sourced from a specialist jewellery-findings manufacturer, or from a serious craft supplier (see the list of suppliers at the end of this book). Jump rings, spacers, beading wire, ear wires, brooch backs, clasps, chains and rigid precious-metal torques are among the findings you can buy.

Findings can be joined to the ceramic part of a piece having a hole or loop, through a cavity or tube, with a claw or bezel setting or by the use of glue. Two-part epoxy glue is recommended by suppliers of findings for joining earring backs and brooch backs to ceramics.

For threading beads, nylon-coated, twisted stainless-steel wire, known as Tigertail or Beadalon, is strong and neat and comes in silver, gold or other colours. Silver or gold crimpers, used in conjunction with Tigertail, can separate beads or be used to aid the making of a loop so that a jump ring or fastener may be affixed (usually three at each end). The crimpers are squeezed together with flat-nose pliers.

A jump ring is put through the end loop, to which is added the fastening clasp at one end, while at the other end there is a larger ring used to complete the fastening. If two or more strands need to be joined together, they are gathered into a single crimper, which is then squeezed to clasp them tightly together. Then, with a dab of two-part epoxy glue, a coulet (a

Ralf Dostmann, beads strung onto Tigertail, with crimpers separating the beads. *Photo: Ralf Dostmann.*

Katrin Jaeger, *Terrassen* necklace, 2008. Ceramic elements, with oxidised silver claw settings and chain from Rashbel UK, l: 90 mm (3½ in.). *Photo: Katrin Jaeger.*

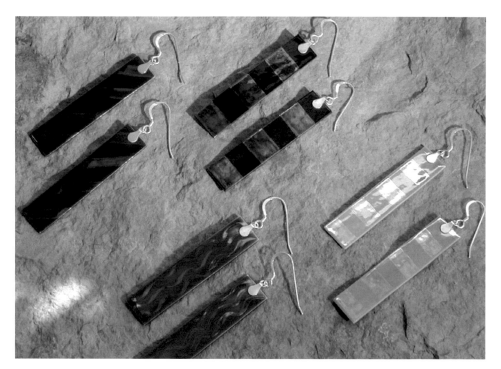

Blake and Janette Mackinnon, oblong earrings. White earthenware glaze fired to 1150°C (2102°F) with mother-of-pearl lustre re-fired to 780°C (1436°F) , 40 × 10 mm (1½ × ⅜ in.) earring wires – from Rashbel UK (see suppliers' list). *Photo: Janette Mackinnon.*

split ball with a ring) is squeezed around the crimper to strengthen and complete the join. The coulet also has a ring to hold the jump ring and fastening clasp. It is also possible to buy fasteners with multiple rings, to which are attached the individual strands.

Katrin Jaeger has used silver claw settings and chain sourced through Rashbel UK. These she has oxidised with potassium sulphide before bringing them together in a creative way with the ceramic elements and a smoky quartz.

In the series of photos (right and on p.82), a simple pair of earrings have been made from individual elements which could be handmade or bought from a jewellery findings supplier. Silver wire is cut to 6 cm (2¼ in.)

Tools for making simple earrings.

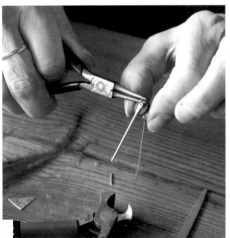

Constructing simple earrings from handmade elements (these pieces can also be bought).

1 Wire cut to length, the ends curled around and through individual components using the round-nosed pliers.

2–3 Round-nose pliers are used to bend and form the wire finding which joins the separate elements together.

4 Filing the cut end of the earring finding.

5 Finished silver earrings with raku bead by Joy Bosworth, 2009.

Photos: Frank Fisher.

ABOVE Four neckpieces: Rachel Wood's hessian string and textured green stoneware *Derbyshire* neckpiece; Joy Bosworth's bound silk and raku-fired irregular bead neckpiece; Sarah Perry and Joy Bosworth's striped lustre medallion with black waxed-cotton and a silver tube toggle; and Sue Crossfield's barium stoneware glazed beads on a waxed cotton yarn with two sliding knots fastening. *Photo: Dan Bosworth.*

long, and one end is curled around and through a hole in the triangular element, to make a ring, using the round-nosed pliers. One end of a shorter wire (2.5 cm/1 in.) is curled around and through the other hole. The bead and dropper element are threaded onto this shorter wire and the last ring is made which holds them all together. The longer wire is now bent back on itself allowing it to be worn in the ear. The length is adjusted by cutting it with a wire cutter and filing, and then it is bent back slightly to complete the earring.

Types of yarns, cords and thonging, and the best fastenings to use with them

Neckpieces, on which the ceramic component hangs, can be bought complete, but it may be desirable to make more individual pieces. Using yarn, ribbon or thonging as a neckpiece, some of which are illustrated above, brings different contrasts to the ceramic elements. Rachel Wood's hessian string links together the textured green medallions, and the fastening is a simple knotted loop with a ceramic toggle. Joy

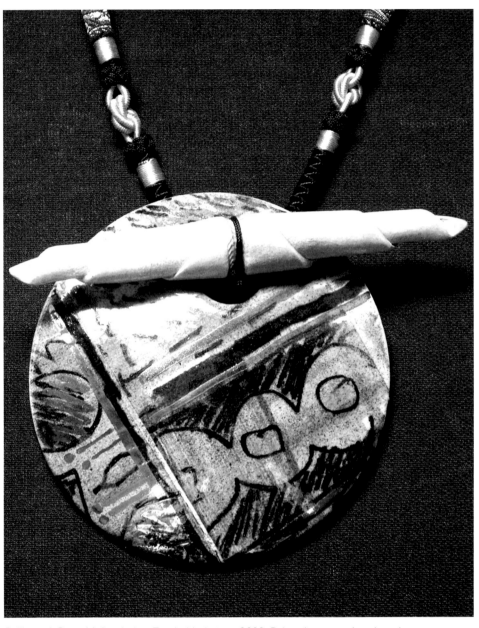

Pollie and Garry Uttley, *Indian Toggle Neckpiece*, 2008. Painted, monoprinted earthenware glazed with lustre. *Photo: Garry Uttley.*

Daisy Choi, *Best Before* Collection, 2008. Oxidized silver and slipcast porcelain egg. *Photo: Daisy Choi.*

Bosworth's bound neckpiece with irregular beads also has a loop-and-bead fastening, but the bound nature of the yarn creates a different quality. In the Sarah Perry/Joy Bosworth piece, a black waxed-cotton thread is used with a silver tube toggle, which slides to allow the length of the neckpiece to change. Finally, Sue Crossfield has used two sliding knots on her neckpiece to allow for a variable length.

The dramatic neckpiece made by Pollie and Garry Uttley makes the toggle fastening a decorative part of the design. The cord, made specially for them in India, completes the professional look of the neckpiece.

Handmade precious-metal findings

You may wonder why you would want to make your own findings when an enormous variety of perfectly good ones can be bought readymade. However, specific, one-off findings can bring together the design of a particular piece with its function, giving it a more individual quality. Gallery owners and some buyers will look at the findings to see if they are both functional and a suitable size and design for the piece; for expensive individual jewellery, they often prefer handmade findings that lend the piece a distinctive quality. The hand-made silver elements in the necklace above by Daisy Choi have been combined with manufactured chain, and the whole

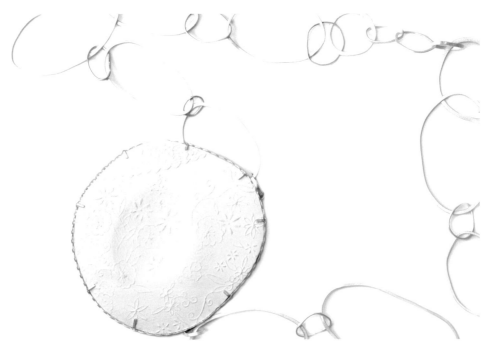

Kathryn Partington, *Pure* neckpiece, (view I). With bone china and silver (cubic zirconium on the back of the piece is unseen). *Photo: Gareth Partington.*

ensemble has been oxidised to unify it so that the findings become part of the overall design. Kathryn Partington also makes her own silver findings to bring a freedom and irregularity to her distinctive silver and bone-china pieces.

T-bar clasp

My piece on p.87 shows how a fastening can become the focus of the design. Here the outsized clasp has been made into a decorative feature. A loop and T-bar clasp has been handmade from a raku-fired loop and a handmade silver chain and bar. The dyed muslin neckpiece has been gathered together into silver cones which have been bent and hammered around a wooden former.

Precious-metal clay findings

Precious-metal clay (PMC) is a substance that combines precious-metal filings with an organic binder. It behaves like putty and, being tricky to model, works well for small items such as findings.

Dawn Michelle van Gerven has made precious-metal clay findings for her flat ceramic pieces (p.88). The porcelain medallion is fired to 1260°C (2300°F) with a glaze, then the silver PMC is rolled into shape, wrapped around the piece of ceramic, fixed with PMC paste, and left to dry. The back of the piece is then built up with PMC paste. A hole is drilled into the dry PMC to take a jump ring. The whole piece is then smoothed, filed and sanded to finish the shape and remove any imperfections. The complete

Joy Bosworth, scarf neckpiece. Unglazed raku-fired ceramic ring with handmade silver T-bar and chain, silver cones and dyed muslin, clasp: 40 × 30 mm (1½ × 1⅛ in.), l: 570 mm (2¼ in.). *Photo: Dan Bosworth.*

The precious-metal clay finding is cleaned.

The precious-metal clay finding is smoothed with an abrasive pad when dry.

Dawn Michelle van Gerven, finished medallions, 2008. Precious-metal clay and glazed, marbled porcelain, each 50 × 25 mm (2 × 1 in.). *Photo: Dawn Michelle van Gerven.*

piece can be fired when dry to between 650 and 800°C (1202 and 1472°F), with the kiln being allowed to 'soak' for between 10 to 30 minutes. To 'soak' a kiln means to maintain it at a specific temperature for a time, to allow a glaze to develop or a specific look to be achieved. In this case it was soaked at 800°C (1472°F) for 30 minutes. This will not damage the part of the medallion which was fired to 1260°C (2300°F), as the lower firing for the PMC does not effect a higher-fired piece. After firing it needs to be brushed with a wire brush to bring out the silver and then polished to a high finish with silver polish. The PMC does shrink a small amount, so a very small amount of space is left between the porcelain and the silver PMC to allow for that.

Isabel Denyer has used precious metal clay to make the cone-shaped findings seen opposite. She has found that forming the PMC over a cone-shaped model, made from magazine paper, makes it much easier to manage the putty-like substance.

RIGHT Isabel Denyer, cone-shaped precious-metal clay finding shown with the magazine paper model. *Photo: Isabel Denyer.*

BELOW Isabel Denyer, necklace, 2008. Precious-metal clay, Egyptian paste, porcelain and raku-fired beads with handmade precious-metal clay and sheet-silver fastener, l: 540 mm (21¼ in.). *Photo: Isabel Denyer.*

More advanced techniques

Lydia Feast's brooch (left) has developed from her interest in composition, and using porcelain and oxidised silver together allows her to contrast the different materials and their different properties. Here the oxidised silver finding protects the porcelain and holds it in place but is also part of the composition. The 0.8mm stainless-steel pins are strong and springy, and pivot from the silver tube, being held in place by the hooks cut out of the brooch-back collar.

Amy Smart's starting point for the brooch (opposite) was her love of decay, the change that occurs in materials with age, which can be beautiful despite having been discarded. She has used red clay, which she has smoked, as well as oxidised silver and patinated copper. Joining the metal elements together by soldering them would have spoiled the patinated surfaces of the metals, so silver tube rivets were used instead. The design of the metal findings was worked out first on thick paper before the metal was cut.

Hannah Miller, as seen opposite, has formed a silver tube from a sheet of silver onto which the porcelain 'doughnut' sits tightly, without any other means of support. The attractive feature of this design is that the ring band is visible inside the circular hole of the porcelain.

Lydia Feast, brooch, 2009. Porcelain and oxidised silver, dia: 50 mm (2 in.). *Photo: Dan Bosworth.*

Lydia Feast, brooch back, 2009. Porcelain and oxidised silver with stainless-steel wire pin, dia: 50 mm (19¾ in.). *Photo: Dan Bosworth.*

Amy Smart, brooch, 2009. Smoked red clay, oxidised silver and patinated copper, 70 × 70 mm (2¾ × 2¾ in.). *Photo: Dan Bosworth.*

Amy Smart, brooch back, 2009. Smoked red clay, oxidised silver and patinated copper with stainless-steel wire pins, 70 × 70 mm (2¾ × 2¾ in.). *Photo: Dan Bosworth.*

Hannah Miller, *Hole Ring*, 2009. Silver and porcelain, dia: 30 mm (1¼ in.). *Photo: Dan Bosworth.*

Chapter 8

Gallery

Sebastian Buescher

Sebastian Buescher's themes have been broad including the past, nature, irony and contradiction, and more recently (through including recycled second-hand objects) he has explored larger subjects like the invisible energy of objects, together with ghosts and the meaning and purpose of being a human being.

Buescher's work brings jewellery into new territory, breaking established traditions. His latest collection, called *Imperfection Please,* is concerned with experimentation and the freedom that allows. During this process, he has become aware that the qualities offered by ceramics reflect some of his own concerns, particularly its fragility, which he sees as a metaphor for the human condition. The pieces have moved away from jewellery and are more concerned with 'meaning and purpose ... capturing emotions, thoughts and ideas' which refer to milestones in his own life.

Sebastian Buescher, untitled brooch, 2007. Body-stained stoneware, plastic, agate, jade, silver and thread, 12 × 12 cm (4³/₄ × 4³/₄ in.). Courtesy of Galerie Rob Koudijs, Amsterdam. *Photo: Sebastian Buescher.*

Daisy Choi

Daisy Choi has attracted the interest of a number of magazines both in the UK and the USA. She shows internationally in galleries and shops in the UK, Europe and the USA. She works with ceramics, precious metals and gemstones, making playful and humorous collections. In the collection *Best Before* 'the egg is symbolic of life refreshed and reborn'.

Daisy Choi, *Best Before* collection, 2008. Slipcast porcelain and oxidised silver, l: 1500 mm (59 in.). Model: Alice Magnin. *Photo: Daisy Choi.*

Aneta Regel Deleu, *Volcanic Ring*, 2008. Porcelain and stoneware clays, feldspars, volcanic rocks and commercial glazes. *Photo: Sylvain Deleu.*

Aneta Regel Deleu

Aneta Regel Deleu's masculine rings juxtapose forms of nature and natural materials with the manmade. She creates objects that exist neither in the natural nor in the manufactured world, but she hopes that they reflect and transmit information about nature and the effect mankind can have on it, both positive and negative. She aims to convey a sense of transformation from one state to another. The contrast of rough and smooth is crucial, and in this case she uses a rich, brightly coloured yellow glaze to 'refer to radioactivity caused naturally and by mankind'.

Aneta Regel Deleu's *Volcanic Ring* was fired first to a stoneware temperature, which gives strength to the porcelain and volcanic rock form, before being fired with commercial glazes to a lower earthenware temperature.

Rebecca Dolby, knitted neckpiece, 2008. Chemical-dyed yarn and raku-fired beads, 75 × 6 cm (29½ × 2¼ in.). *Photo: Dan Bosworth.*

Rebecca Dolby

Rebecca Dolby has incorporated raku-fired loops made by Joy Bosworth in her neckpiece (shown above).

Her main interest lies in the structure of organic forms and, in this instance, microbiological images of cells. She chose the textile technique (French knitting) to reflect the linear quality of the source images as well as to echo the complex, interwoven structure of the cells.

The yarn chosen is lightweight, in order to be comfortable for the wearer, but dense enough to maintain its form. This is further enhanced by the ceramic components, which give weight and shape to the piece. Her choice of colour was based on vivid chemical dyes, which refer to the colours seen under the microscope and provide a contrast to the piece's more natural overall form.

Lauren Griffiths

Lauren Griffiths has collected found objects since she was a child, scouring pavements and beaches for treasures. She has always found beauty in small objects, whether manmade and discarded or else from nature. The piece shown here (right) has come from her 'diary' of found objects, and reminds her of one beautiful day spent with a friend, beachcombing on the Isle of Wight.

Lauren Griffiths, *Beautiful* brooch, 2009. Porcelain with driftwood and silver, 70 × 40 mm (2¾ × 15¾ in.). *Photo: Dan Bosworth.*

Claire Ireland

Claire Ireland has always been inspired by contemporary jewellery, especially work that is pushing the boundaries of practicality with unconventional use of materials, and very sculptural in concept. She says, 'This sort of approach I find exciting, and it has linked into my decision recently to direct my own work towards a more sculptural and less narrative way of working.'

Sculptors and painters such as Brancusi, Torres García and Calder have always been a major influence throughout her career. David Nash's show at Tate St Ives she found truly inspirational, while Victor Pasmore's constructions and Ben Nicholson's paintings have helped to build up a wealth of ideas that is starting to filter into the new work.

Looking back through her sketchbooks has informed Ireland's research for her jewellery and has helped her realise that these sculptural influences have affected her design and drawing for jewellery. Drawing is a crucial part of the design process, enabling her to refine and adapt the pieces she makes. As a regular visitor to the Pitt Rivers Collection in Oxford and the British Museum in London, she also has a strong interest in tribal artifacts.

Her aim is to make small simple sculptural forms that can be worn in different ways and yet can also be seen as small works of art.

Ireland says that working on her jewellery has given her 'the opportunity to be more experimental with materials and firing methods, using what was available in the studio. I started by carving coloured slipcast earthenware from solid blocks at the leatherhard stage. On some I drew in water-soluble

Claire Ireland, *untitled brooch*. Slipcast white earthenware, saggar-fired using sawdust, copper wire and seaweed, 60 × 80 mm (2⅜ × 3⅛ in.). *Photo: Claire Ireland.*

crayons, sort of wrapping the lines round the fired forms, and sealed them with matt varnish. On others I stamped a pattern in acrylic varnish and sponged away the background at leatherhard stage to reveal an embossed surface.'

She applied a variety of paint-on glazes (fired in the range 1015–1060°C/ 1859–1940°F) together in combination, using a sponge-printing, wax-resist technique (sponge stamps carved with a hot, fine soldering tool). All the forms were finely sanded with wet & dry sandpaper at biscuit stage to give a polished surface, and a selection were wrapped in copper wire, seaweed, or moss and sawdust, and fired in saggars. She has found her jewellery-making experiments a positive experience and a beneficial creative tool to use in working towards larger pieces.

Tanvi Kant

Tanvi Kant uses 'fabrics reclaimed from family and friends which are evocative of personal and often private histories'. She contrasts the high-fired porcelain rings with the soft nature of the fabric. She is inspired by the hand-stitched hem of her mother's silk saris, and began by using threads unpicked from reclaimed textiles to sew around strips torn from the same fabrics. By whipping, binding, knotting and sewing the sari silk, the process of making develops in response to the materials she uses. Her attempts to protect the fragility of the torn fragments of textile reflect a determination to cherish the stories they embody.

Tanvi Kant, *Chunky Blue*, 2007. Tangled neckpiece with bound antique sari silk and porcelain links. *Photo: Tas Kyprianou.*

Mervi Kervinen, *Las Palmas Geisha Balls*, 2007. Still from the video installation *Greetings from Paradise Found*, by Kimmo Heikila.

Mervi Kervinen

Mervi Kervinen, the Finnish artist and teacher, makes artefacts from ceramics and other materials which she includes in video installations. *Las Palmas Geisha Balls* is one of the pieces that she made combining the kitsch souvenir theme and delicate crafts. She likes to combine different kinds of worlds, such as the opposing ideas of mass production and the unique object. *Las Palmas Geisha Balls* contains porcelain with hand-painted flower images and a silver chain. It deals with sexual and humorous feelings. Kervinen likes to connect an object and a person together and to create an environment and a place for the pieces.

Kathryn Partington, *Pure Necklace*. Bone china and silver, l: 900 mm (35½ in.). *Photo: Gareth Partington.*

Kathryn Partington

Kathryn Partington is interested in the application of surface pattern and ornamentation in jewellery, and uses her experience in designing tableware and surface pattern for Wedgwood, and in printed textiles, to further develop her skills through manipulating and experimenting with materials in making jewellery pieces.

Her use of decoration arises from the deconstruction and reconstruction of an 1890 Victorian adaptation of a Japanese-style tableware pattern. She says, 'I see my work as an evolutionary process that, informed by the Japanese aesthetic, uses hand-drawing, engraving, slip-casting techniques and print development, each process acting as a tool aiming to integrate these influences.' She re-creates, evolves and makes reference to the past, while the manipulations of her various processes contain echoes of the original that will always remain. Although her work references the past, it is contemporary in nature.

Ruudt Peters

The Dutch jeweller Ruudt Peters's work is challenging on many levels, not least in his subject matter and combinations of materials. In his collection called *Lingam* he responds to the South-east Asian tradition of men wearing a talisman inside their underwear as a devotion to fertility. Pieces from the *Lingam* series are intended to be worn by men as body adornment around the waist.

Peters worked for three months in 2001 with EKWC, the European Ceramics Work Centre in Den Bosch, in the Netherlands, where he made the porcelain objects which are then combined with wood and red coral in his fertility pieces.

Ruudt Peters, *Lingam 3*, 2007. Wood, ceramics, red coral, 360 × 160 × 160 mm (14¼ × 6¼ × 6¼ in.). *Photo: Ruudt Peters.*

Karin Seufert, untitled, 2003. Two brooches, cut and reassembled china object, colorit, enamel with silver, (also amethyst on the right-hand brooch). *Photo: Karin Seufert.*

Karin Seufert

The German jewellery maker Karin Seufert told me 'When I was at Rietveld Academy I had a professor called Marion Herbst who died quite young. In 2002, I had an exhibition at Galerie Marzee in Nijmegen [in the Netherlands], and later the former husband of Marion Herbst contacted me and asked if I would like to make a deal with him: one piece of my jewellery from this exhibition in exchange for a box full of material collected by Marion herself. That was fantastic, and for me the beginning of working with found objects.'

The found objects which are seen in these two brooches came out of this box and were the beginning of a whole series. Since then Karin has preferred to work with used objects because of their ability to engage with narrative, memory and meaning.

Ruth Tomlinson

Ruth Tomlinson's work is inspired by the idea of life cycles, from birth to decay, and by transience and change in nature. She says that she likes to respond to her immediate environment and is open to spontaneous finds and observations during the making process. 'Working directly with nature, developing an ongoing relationship and documenting through photographs helps me to achieve a sensitivity to materials within my work.'

Ruth states that had it not been for the treasured bone tools handed down from her grandmother, a keen amateur ceramicist, she might not have developed her porcelain jewellery. 'I have always loved those tools, and it is only now, looking at their distinctive conical shapes, that I realise how fundamental they were in the creation of my ceramic flowers.'

Ruth Tomlinson, *Cluster Rings*, 2002. Gold, oxidised silver and body-stained porcelain, 23 mm (⅞ in.). *Photo: Ruth Tomlinson.*

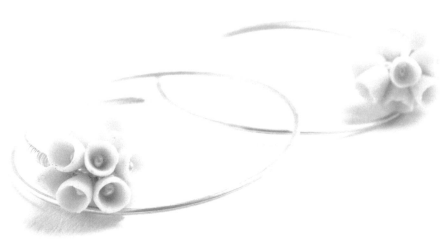

Ruth Tomlinson, *Loop Earrings*, 2009. Silver with porcelain, dia: 4 cm (1½ in.). *Photo: Ruth Tomlinson.*

Health & Safety

Makers should always be aware of health and safety matters, and when working with different materials should be aware of potential hazards, these are usually described in manufacturers catalogues, on packaging or by requesting information from the manufacturer when ordering. Working with clay and glazes, with kilns or with jewellery-making equipment is not in itself dangerous if common sense prevails and manufacturers guidelines are followed. But you should take great care so that accidents do not occur.

Obviously, children should be closely overseen by a trained adult in workshop situations where there may be potentially dangerous or hazardous materials or equipment.

Clay and glazes contain silica, which when dry takes the form of a hazardous dust. Workshops should not be swept as it will create dangerous airborne particles, instead they should be kept clean with wet-wiping or by vacuum-cleaning. Workshops should be well-lit, and well-ventilated. Clean protective clothing should be worn in the pottery studio or workshop, and dust masks should always be worn when glaze-spraying or carrying out any procedure that creates dust or airborn silica

particles. Glaze-spraying should only be done in a suitable extraction unit.

Always wear goggles or safety glasses when using high-speed polishing equipment and drills. Always tie back long hair and avoid wearing loose clothing which could get caught in equipment.

Certain toxic materials must not be inhaled or ingested, and with this in mind you should always follow the manufacturer's instructions for any material you are using. Always comply with the hazard labels and instructions that accompany particular substances, and keep hazardous chemicals in sealed and marked containers. Chemicals should be kept out of the reach of children and in a cool place.

Care should be taken with gas bottles and with sources of heat for kilns or jewellery torches. Fumes given off from firing kilns can be toxic, so good ventilation and adequate extraction is very important. Electric kilns should always be installed by a specialist electrician. Gas torches should be turned off at the bottle to prevent leaks. Heat-resistant gloves should be worn when firing and unpacking kilns.

Never eat, drink or smoke in the workshop.

Bibliography

Birks, T., *A Complete Guide to Pottery-making Techniques* (A & C Black, 1988).

Bosworth, Joy, *Ceramics with Mixed Media* (A & C Black, 2006).

Codina i Armengol, Carles, *The New Jewelery: Contemporary Materials and Techniques* (Lark Books, 2005).

Connell, Jo, *Colouring Clay* (A & C Black, 2007).

de Kegel, Cecile & Oei, Loan, *The Elements of Design* (Thames and Hudson, 2002).

Genders, Carolyn, *Sources of Inspiration* (A & C Black, 2002).

Grant, Linda, 'V & A's New Jewellery Gallery: Rocks of Ages', *Sunday Telegraph* supplement, 11 May 2008.

Gregory, Ian, *Kiln Building* (2nd rev. edn) (A & C Black, 2002).

Hardy, Michael, *Handbuilding* (A & C Black, 2006).

McCreight, Tim, *Fundamentals of Metalsmithing* (A & C Black, 1998).

McCreight, Tim, *Precious Metal Clay Techniques* (A & C Black, 2007).

McCreight, Tim, *Working with Precious Metal Clay* (A & C Black, 2000).

McGrath, Jinks, *Basic Jewellery-making Techniques* (Quantum Books, 1993).

Perryman, Jane, *Smoke Firing* (A&C Black, 2008)

Turner, Ralph, Statement in Catalogue *Schmuck,* 2008, Editor: Wolfgang Lösche, (Danner-Stiftung Müchen, 2008).

Von Dassow, Sumi, *Low Firing and Burnishing* (A&C Black, 2009).

Wicks, Sylvia, *The Jewellery-making Manual* (McDonalds Press, 1985).

Suppliers

UK
General jewellery-making and craft supplies

Fred Aldous Ltd
37 Lever Street
Manchester
M1 1LW
www.fredaldous.co.uk
Tel (order line): +44 (0)870 7517300
Tel: +44 (0)161 2364224

Specialist Crafts Ltd
PO Box 247
Leicester
LE1 9QS
www.specialistcrafts.co.uk
Telephone: + 44 (0)1162 697711
Email: info@specialistcrafts.co.uk

Modelling mesh in aluminium, copper or brass, papers, adhesives, paints

Atlantis European Ltd
7–9 Plumbers Row
London
E1 1EQ
www.atlantisart.co.uk
Tel: +44 (0)207 377 8855

Wire suppliers

Faye Metals Ltd
Unit 1, 37 Colville Road
Alton, London
W3 8BL
Ferrous and non-ferrous metal wire.

K.C. Smith Ltd
Cranbourne Road
Potters Bar
Herts.
EN6 3JL
Tel: +44 (0)1600 713227
No website
Stainless-steel wire.

Scientific Wire Co.
18 Raven Road,
South Woodford,
London
E18 8HW
Craft sales: www.wires.co.uk
www.scientificwire.com
Tel: +44 (0)208 505 0002
Email dan@wires.co.uk
Dental steel wire.

Stephen Simpson Ltd
Aveham Road Works
Preston
PR1 3UH
Copper and silver wire.

Jewellery-tools and precious-metal findings

Cookson Precious Metals
59–83 Vittoria Street
Birmingham
B1 3NZ
www.cookson.gold.com
Tel: +44 (0)845 100 1122/
(0)121 200 2120
www.cooksongold.com

Also at:
Cookson and Exchange Findings
49 Hatton Garden
Clerkenwell
London
EC1N 8YS
Tel: +44 (0) 207 400 6500

Cousins Tool Centre
41 Warstone Lane
Hockley
Birmingham
B18 6JJ
Tel +44 (0) 1212 375600
www.cousinsuk.com

Rashbel UK
24–28 Hatton Wall
London
EC1N 8JB
Tel: +44 (0)207 831 5646
www.rashbel.co.uk

Slimbrand
65–66 Warstone Lane
Hockley
Birmingham
B18 6NG
Tel:+44 (0)121 212 2560
www.slimbrand.co.uk
'Precision products in precious metals.'

T.H. Findings Ltd
42 Hylton Street
Hockley
Birmingham
B18 6HN
Tel: +44 (0)121 554 9889
E mail: sales@thfindings.com
www.thfindings.com

Beads and findings

The Bead Loft
1st Floor
53A Frederick Street
Birmingham
B1 3HS
Tel: +44 (0)1212129132
www.thebeadloft.co.uk
(Also offers jewellery-making courses.)

PJ Minerals
583c Liverpool Road
Southport
PR8 3LU
Tel: +44 (0)1704 575461
email: info@beads.co.uk
www.beads.co.uk

Precious-metal clay

Silver Alchemy Supplies
2 Marshall Street
London
W1F 9BB
www.silveralchemy.com

Precious-metal suppliers

Betts Metal Sales Ltd
49–63 Spencer Street
Hockley, Birmingham
B18 6DE
Tel: +44 (0)121 2332413
www.bettsmetals.co.uk

Cookson Precious Metals Ltd
59–83 Vittoria Street
Birmingham
B1 8NZ
Tel: +44 (0)845 100 1122/
(0)121 200 2120
www.cooksongold.com

Clays, glazes, potters tools

Bath Potters' Supplies
Unit 18
Fourth Avenue
Westfield Trading Estate
Radstock
BA3 4XE
Tel: +44 (0)1761 411077
www.bathpotters.demon.co.uk

Potclays
Brick Kiln Lane
Etruria
Stoke-on-Trent
ST4 7BP
sales@potclays.co.uk
Also distributor of Spectrum microwave kiln.

Potterycrafts Ltd
Campbell Road
Stoke-on-Trent
ST4 4ET
Tel: +44 (0)1782 745000
www.potterycrafts.co.uk

Valentine Clays
The Slip House
18–20 Chell Street
Hanley
Stoke-on-Trent
ST1 6BA
Tel: +44 (0)1782 271800
www.valentineclays.co.uk

Kilns

Cromartie Ltd
Park Hall Road
Longton
Stoke-on-Trent
ST3 5AY
Tel: +44 (0)1782 319435

Kilns and Furnaces
Keele Street Works
Tunstall
Stoke-on-Trent
ST6 5AS
Tel: +44 (0)1782 813621

Laser Kilns
Unit C9, Angel Road Works
Advent Way
London
E18 3AH
Tel: +44 (0)208 803 1016
www.laserkilns.co.uk

Potclays
Brick Kiln Lane
Etruria
Stoke-on-Trent
ST4 7BP
sales@potclays.co.uk
Supplier of Spectrum microwave kilns.

US
Tools & materials suppliers (jewellery)

Freecrafts Network Online
www.allcrafts.net/jewelry

Armstrong Tool & Supply Company
31541 West Eight Mile Road
Livonia
M1 48152
Tel: +1 (800) 446-9694
Email: armstool@hotmail.com
www.armstrongtool.com

Beadalon
www.beadalon.com
Tel: (toll-free) 1 (866) 423 2325
Email: sales@beadalon.com
USA manufacturer of jewellery-making wire

Metalliferous
Store: 34 West 46th Street
New York, NY 10036
Tel: +1 (212) 944 0909
Email: info@metalliferous.com
Mail order: 640 South Fulton Avenue,
Mount Vernon, NY 10550
Tel: (toll free) +1 (888) 944 0909
www.metalliferous.com

Rio Grande
Online only
www.riogrande.com
Jewellery-making products.

SWEST Inc.
Online only
www.swestinc.com
Jewellery-making products.

Thompson Enamel Inc.
650 Colfax Ave, Belleview,
KY 41072 USA
Tel (859) 2291 3800
www.thompsonenamel.com

US and Canadian pottery suppliers

Aftosa
1032 Ohio Avenue
Richmond
CA 94804
Tel: +1 (800) 231 0397
www.aftosa.com

American Art Clay Co.
W. 16th Street
Indianapolis
IN 46222
Tel: +1 (317) 244 6871
www.amaco.com

Duncan Colors
3300 Girard NE
Albuquerque
NM 87107
Tel: +1 (505) 881 2350
www.duncanpaintstore.com

Gare, Inc.
165 Rosemont Street
Haverhill
MA 01832-1340
Tel: +1 (978) 373 9131
www.gare.com

Laguna Clay Co.
1440 Lomitas Avenue
City of Industry
CA 91746
Tel: +1 (800) 452 4862
www.lagunaclay.com

Mayco Colors
4077 Weaver Court South
Hilliard
OH 43026
Tel: +1 (614) 876 1171
info@maycocolors.com
www.maycocolors.com

Minnesota Clay Co.
8001 Grand Avenue South
Bloomington
MN 55420
Tel: +1 (612) 884 9101

Tuckers Pottery Supplies Inc.
15 West Pearce Street
Richmond Hill
Ontario
Canada, L4B 1H6
Tel: +1 (800) 304 6185
www.tuckerspottery.com

Glossary

Anneal To heat materials and allow them to cool slowly in order to remove internal stresses. Metal needs to be annealed regularly during forming to make it malleable. Glass needs to be annealed during firing otherwise it will crack.

Body stain A manufactured powder using colour clay or slip.

Borax A flux used by jewellers to aid soldering, it comes in a solid cone and, when ground with water, forms a milky consistency.

Burnishing To polish the surface of almost dry clay before firing with a smooth stone or the back of a spoon.

Cast A way to duplicate objects by pouring liquid materials into a mould.

Casting slip A liquid clay combining clay, water and a deflocculant, used for casting into a mould.

Celadon A type of reduced stoneware glaze which uses small amounts of iron to create a pale-green colour.

Colorit A reinforced ceramic composite used by jewellers with the feel of enamel, but which needs no heat or kiln to cure.

Cottle A wall used in mould-making to encase a model. Liquid Plaster of Paris is poured into the space between the wall and the model to make a mould for casting.

Crimpers Tiny, soft precious-metal tubes which are squeezed over Tigertail to hold beads in position or to hold the ends into a loop to receive a fastening.

Dye plate A template made from metal or Perspex with a cut shape, through which the clay is pushed as it comes out of the extruder.

Egyptian paste A combination of clay, glaze and soluble salts which during drying allows the glaze material to rise to the surface, appearing as surface crystals. The glaze is formed when fired to 870°C (1598°F).

Electroplating The process, using electrolysis, of depositing a thin layer of metal over another material for decorative or practical reasons.

Enamel A ceramic substance which creates colour on top of a glaze at low temperatures in a third firing.

Extruder A machine through which clay is forced, with the use of a dye plate, to create decorative shapes.

Files Used in metalwork in different sizes and shapes for refining shapes, removing solder and levelling surfaces.

Finding The mechanics of a piece of jewellery, it allows different parts to be joined together into a functional piece that can be worn.

Glass A brittle, usually transparent material made by fusing together sand, soda, lime and sometimes other ingredients.

Hammer Different types are needed to strike metal for a range of jewellery purposes including forming, texturing and planishing.

Inlay A decorative technique whereby coloured slip fills depressions in the clay surface, which is scraped back when dry to reveal the pattern inlaid into the surface.

Jeweller's peg or pin A small wooden wedge, permanently fixed to a table or else with a G-clamp, into which a V shape is cut to enable work to be supported during sawing, filing, cleaning, etc.

Marbling A decorative technique in which two or more different-coloured clays are partly kneaded together.

Modelling A technique to produce three-dimensional or relief pieces in clay by building up the form using small pieces of clay.

Mould Made in one or more parts, usually in plaster of Paris, it is used to quickly replicate the same shape in clay.

Nichrome wire Sometimes known as Kanthal wire, it can withstand great heat, and can be used to suspend beads in a kiln.

Oxidised silver Silver blackened with a chemical.

Oxides Minerals used to colour glazes and the clay surface.

Patinate To alter the colour of metal through oxidisation with chemicals or heat.

Pallion A tiny square of solder used when joining two metals with heat.

Pendant Motor A portable rotating motor which hangs above the work bench and takes different jewellery tools for polishing, drilling, or texturing etc.

Pickle Dilute sulphuric acid used to clean metal after soldering.

Piercing saw A fine saw used by jewellers, with disposable blades of different grades.

Plaster of Paris A white powder which, when mixed with water, hardens to be used in mould-making.

Plastic Mallet A hammer-like tool used for forming, which does not damage the surface of metal.

Pliers (round-nose, square-nose) Pincers with different jaws for holding or bending metal or wire.

Precious-metal clay (PMC) A combination of an organic binder and powdered precious metal, which can be modelled as clay and fired to produce a 99% precious-metal product.

Rivet A metal tube which is pushed through holes in one or more layers of metal, the ends of which are spread to hold the separate layers firmly.

Rouge Greasy polish used with a pendant motor or polisher when polishing jewellery.

Roulette A tool which rolls over the surface of clay to create a texture.

Scribe A sharp metal tool, used for marking metal.

Slip Liquid clay.

Slipcasting A method for making repeated forms using casting slip and a mould.

Slab-building A method for making forms with sheets of clay.

Silver solder Silver alloy which when heated with borax melts and joins together two pieces of metal.

Solder To join together two or more pieces of metal using borax flux and pallions of solder, with heat being applied equally to each piece.

Sprig A small raised clay decoration, usually made in a mould, applied to the surface of a clay object with slip.

Throwing A way of making clay objects on a potter's wheel.

Tigertail Plastic-coated stainless-steel wire.

Torch There are different sizes for different jobs: smaller ones fuelled by lighter fuel or propane gas for jewellery-soldering, or larger ones fuelled by propane gas for firing small kilns.

Wire cutters A hand tool for cutting wire.

Index